Coast-to-Coasting

coast-to-coasting

Eight coast-to-coast walks crossing Britain

JOHN GILLHAM AND RONALD TURNBULL

David & Charles

A DAVID & CHARLES BOOK

Publisher: Pippa Rubinstein
Commissioning editor: Sue Viccars
Art editor: Sue Cleave
Designer: Les Dominey
Production: Beverley Richardson

First published in the UK in 2000

ISBN 0 7153 0955 2

Colour origination by Global Colour
Printed in Italy
by MILANOSTAMPA
for David & Charles
Brunel House
Newton Abbot   Devon

Jacket photographs: (*front*) Reaching
the coast at Durdle Door on Uphill to
Old Harry; (*back, left*) Dawn over Glen
Dessarry on a crossing of the Scottish
Highlands; (*back, right*) Glowylyn in the
Rhinogs on Snowdonia to Gower

Half-title page: Sea and Skye from
Sgurr na Feartaig
Title page: Snowdon sunset
right: Looking down to Wasdale Head

Contents

Introduction

The best walks go all the way across!

Start with the sea-cliffs of Dorset or Yorkshire. Here the wild weather, crags and narrow paths of mountain country are brought conveniently down to the zero contour and enriched with crashing surf and sandy beaches. Walk a gentle coastal plain, and the first of twenty mossy woods. Play hunt-the-stile for half a day across the cow-pastures.

Then, perhaps, the Pennines: and the Pennines not as a place to drive into and do a little circular walk, but the Pennines as a huge obstacle lying across the path. Or not the Pennines but the Eastern Grampians, or the mountains of Snowdonia. Cross the stony or peaty plateau, under whatever weather it feels like throwing at you, and at dusk descend to an unknown valley and the lights of an inn. Meet the landlady you spoke to on the phone a fortnight ago, from some city office or suburban hallway or even on your horrid mobile.

The original coast-to-coast, and certainly one of the best, is **Wainwright's Coast-to-Coast** ('The Coast-to-Coast'). Going bang through the middle of three great upland areas, it is guaranteed good hill-walking. More, the hill-walking is good in three different ways, as the walk passes from the North York Moors, through Swaledale, to its climax in the Lake District.

This is probably Britain's most popular long-distance route, and rightly so. It has a balance of the wild and the civilised that's just right for ordinary walkers on their first long walk. It has some tough days, but every night is a comfortable one in an inn, B&B or youth hostel. It has the proper complement of woods, waterfalls and footbridges. It is challenging, but not too challenging, and its 190 miles (300km) take a fortnight, which is a convenient period of time.

The aim of our book will be to convince you, by words and by pictures, that there are other walks of this calibre in the British Isles. Many of our readers will already have completed the Wainwright Coast-to-Coast, and will be looking for something similar – something similar but shorter – or something just as good but a bit more challenging.

In a recent survey by *Strider*, the magazine of the Long Distance Walkers' Association, the title of 'Best Long-distance Path' was shared by Wainwright's Coast-to-Coast and the **Offa's Dyke Path**. This one is the only National Trail (indeed, the only waymarked route) in our book. Here are no popular hills (apart from the Clwydian Range), but a quiet country of upland and valley. Its 170 miles (280km) can be covered comfortably in ten days or a fortnight, and Offa's Dyke is a sensible sort of walk in other ways as well. Modern civilisation seems distant in this under-populated country, and yet its happier manifestations, such as B&Bs and beer, occur as often as required. The line of the ancient Dyke lends a historical rationale to a walk that really doesn't require such added justification.

The **Snowdonia to Gower** coast-to-coast route takes Wales more seriously, choosing to head for the bigger, rockier mountains of the National Parks. It seeks out the highest tops like Snowdon and Cadair Idris, but, for the days when it rains or when you're just a bit under the weather

right: Eastern Carneddau from the slopes of Moel Siabod

overleaf: Llyn Cau from Cadair Idris. Snowdonia to Gower combines the famous mountains of North Wales with equally wild but less well-known country of the South

above: Britain's seaside scenery is one reason why coast-to-coast is the best sort of walk. The last 25 miles (40km) of Uphill to Old Harry follow the Dorset coastline, seen here at Swyre Head

opposite: Where it all started. Descending into Borrowdale on the Coast-to-Coast route devised by Alfred Wainwright

yourself, it offers low-level alternatives that take in the valleys and the passes. Sometimes it just feels better and more logical to thread through the mountains rather than over them.

Snowdonia to the Gower also seeks out that bit of Wales in the middle; the green bit nobody bothers with. Walkers on this route will remember this green bit: it's the bit where the roaring torrents of Elan thunder down huge stone-built dams; it's the bit where unknown splintered cliffs look down on crystal streams and oakwoods; and it's the bit where you can spend two days without seeing another walker.

Uphill to Old Harry is a greener and gentler sort of coast-to-coast walk: a good one for spring or autumn, or for when you've only a week to walk in. It offers the limestone Mendips with Cheddar Gorge and the small hills of Somerset, then the chalk ridges and the impolite hill-carving at Cerne Abbas, and finishes along the famous Dorset coast. It offers exercise but also education, for it's a worked example of the 'do-it-yourself' walk made from bits of existing paths, with the Explorer maps as instruction manuals, and the rights-of-way as string to tie together the bits that wouldn't fit.

A proper coast-to-coast crossing of Scotland takes in both **Highland and Grampian**: both Wester Ross and the hills of Aberdeen. This is the big one. To the difficulties of 250 miles (400km), mountain all the way, are added: a heavy pack, as camping out is almost obligatory; bogs and midges at low level, and June blizzards at altitude; crossings of rain-swollen rivers; and the selection, and finding, of a route – for there is no single 'Scottish Coast-to-Coast'. The route we've given here is a relatively simple starter. It crosses by twelve high passes, rather than over the mountaintops, and has a roof of sorts for every night of the crossing.

Lakeland to Lindisfarne, like Wainwright's Coast-to-Coast, goes from the Cumbrian Coast to the North Sea. Its low-level route requires about the same level of fitness, although the mountain route, which tackles Scafell Pike and Cross Fell, is more serious. Outside the Lakes, while Wainwright opted for more pretty paths in another two National Parks, Lakeland to Lindisfarne heads north-east for the more subtle pleasures of the high Pennines and the stark heather moors of Hexhamshire. After all that time in the wilderness, it gets greedy for coast and castles and spends over 20 miles (30km) on the sand or on cliff-tops, taking in the old fortresses of Dunstanburgh, Bamburgh and Lindisfarne.

North of Inverness the roads shrink to single track and peter out. This is the wild part of our island; the crossing of it may be short but it is very serious. On the way from **Beauly to Applecross** we cross fourteen mountains, but only one inhabited valley. This is a route of heather slopes and long mossy ridges. It camps high beside a sparkling lochan, threads a precipice and camps beside another lochan. It scrambles onto the stony plateau of Beinn Bhan and watches the sun go down behind the Isle of Skye. At 80 miles (130km) it may be the least long in the book, but it's no short walk when you cross to Applecross.

The whole point of exploring is that you don't know what you're going to get. A route through **Northern Ireland** from the mountains of Mourne through Antrim's nine glens to the Giant's Causeway was wonderful in some ways but wouldn't quite work overall. So we walk **North to the Forth**, and cross the gentle but (to most of us) strange ranges of Lowther and Culter, the Broughton Heights and the Pentlands, to finish in style along the Royal Mile.

Offa's Dyke, Uphill to Old Harry, and the valley versions of Snowdonia to Gower and Lakes to Lindisfarne can be described as low-level routes. Though map-reading skills are desirable, if you get lost due to lack of such skills you'll suffer inconvenience but not permanent injury or death.

above: Linking mountain to mountain all the way across ... Sgurr Choinnich from Sgurr a' Chaorachain (Beauly to Applecross)

The other routes are mountain ones and some previous experience of hill-walking is advisable, together with hill-type clothing and equipment. Highland and Grampian should not be undertaken as a first long-distance walk, and Beauly to Applecross perhaps not even as a second one. Get it wrong on Uphill to Old Harry and pay for your mistake with sore legs and nettled knees. Get it wrong on Beauly to Applecross and you pay with your life.

Chase your food across 20 miles (30km) of rough country, and go as hungry as an unsuccessful elk hunter because you forgot the shop closes on Sunday. Experience deep heather in the dark; unexpected snow showers on the Great Moss of the Cairngorms; high winds on an over-ambitious scramble on Scafell Pike. In the civilised twenty-first century, this is about as real as it gets.

It isn't possible to do 1300 miles (2000km) of ground in guidebook detail in a single volume (and the authors have already written detailed guidebooks for three of the walks). The routes are described so as to be traced onto a walkers' map, with additional navigation detail on the four that have not previously appeared in print.

May and June are the best months for British walking. At other times of year there is a high likelihood of long outbreaks of rain, excessive heat, snow and ice, midges, early darkness, closed

B&Bs or excessively soggy paths – though even our lively climate shouldn't give every one of these problems within a single crossing.

Most of the walks have been designed to be done without tent, for those who prefer not to carry immensely heavy loads for days and days on end. These walks are much more enjoyable than lying on some Spanish sand smearing yourself with Factor Five. Don't try to make them also cheaper than Spain. Spend some money in B&Bs and bars, and appreciate that you are bringing revenue to parts of the country that badly need it.

From the Vale of Eden to the Loch of Hell; from the heights of the Pont Cysyllte Viaduct to the depths of Wookey Hole; these walks are as varied as Britain itself. They have just three things in common.

They all start at the sea. They all end at the sea.
And they all go all the way across.

above: Somerset sunset on Uphill to Old Harry. Constant switching from the fierce to the pretty, from countryside to mountainside and back again, gives coast-to-coast walking its particular richness

overleaf: Leaving Loch Ailort at the start of a walk to Aberdeen. Any high-level crossing of Scotland is serious – and seriously good

North Sea to Irish Sea

Wainwright's Coast-to-Coast

Three Days to Kidsty Pike

Everest is nice and big – but in other ways, Everest is a nuisance. Everest makes you buy expensive downy clothing, Everest gives you altitude sickness and frostbite, Everest means you have to make friends with yaks. Worst of all, Everest is inconveniently sited – not in England's Lake District.

However, there is one Lakeland summit that, taken by its standard and most popular route, does require a total of 28,000ft (8800m) of ascent. It does require the approach march through range beyond range of foothills. It does require planning, and supply dumps, and long days in monsoon weather when a tactless remark to a tentmate will imperil the whole expedition. And a really well-developed British blister hurts much, much more than mere frostbite ….

THE APPROACH MARCH

The short way up Kidsty Pike is from Haweswater. But I was doing Kidsty Pike the Himalayan way – the Wainwright Coast-to-Coast way. The moon made long silver streaks across the North Sea as I lay thinking over the four days ahead of the ascent of Kidsty Pike. But my grassy hollow was so cosy that I fell asleep, just below the wind and lulled by the faint crashing of the waves, before I'd really started worrying about the arduous days ahead, or even finished enjoying the huge moon that rose behind the thorns, the orange-and-black sea scenery.

This attempt on the eight-thousander was to be in the 'Alpine style': lightweight and unencumbered. The discomfort of the bivvy bag makes for early starts and long days. Beside me, upside-down to keep out the dew, lay my hillrunning shoes – but any hillrunning was going to be of the slowest sort. Trot-and-linger was to be the rhythm of the trip, for the long approach-march to Kidsty Pike has many places to linger in, as well as the odd one that should be discreetly trotted over.

The dawn caravan site has a tarred street through, with orange street-lamps: is this really a mountaineering expedition? The sleeping village scarcely reassures, and the heather moor, when it comes, has large lorries driving along the crest above … but then I got lost in Littlebeck.

Littlebeck is a wild wood dropping into a stream. There's a path, but it's a path between brambles and under rocks, with a crumbling earth edge, and other paths with confusing waymarks that dash off sideways into swamps. This is real walking

of an archaic, Bronze Age sort: civilised Romans take to the open hilltops, but barbarian walkers go through the woods and take three times as long. Littlebeck is better, but alas, Littlebeck is little…. All too soon I was up and over into Eskdale.

Eskdale is pretty. Eskdale has a pretty little steam railway, and a pretty little set of stepping stones, perfectly placed to let you cross quite dry-shod, and then wade out into the river trying to take the photo of them. Eskdale has a pretty little bridge where you stop and buy an ice-cream. In Eskdale the green leaves are springing … wouldn't I be better ascending Kidsty Pike from Hartsop, say, or the Kirkstone?

The advantage of doing things quickly is that it doesn't take so long to get the point. This walk of Wainwright's is in twelve bits, and the bits are all different. Eskdale is the pretty bit that helps you appreciate the North York Moors. The North York Moors are flat and brown and fast, with green valleys vanishing into haze on every side. Flat and fast is hard for hillrunners as we normally walk the uphill bits, and that's a nice rest, but here there are no uphill bits.

The long track over the moors is decorated with misshapen lumps. Those in the heather alongside are standing stones, seventeenth-century waymarks. Those actually on the gravel are fellow-walkers, most of whom are on their long, triumphant descent off Kidsty Pike or else going up it like me. And look! Here comes a fellow-runner. I turn, drop the sack and run alongside. How delightfully fast and fresh one feels alongside someone with a bad leg or two who's just come down off Kidsty. For this man, along with five friends, has been attempting the record for

above: 'Highest i' all Yorkshire' according to legend – Roseberry Topping is here seen, from Clay Bank Top, pretending to be an active volcano. This small but pointed hill stands at the edge of the North York Moors, looking across the wide Vale of Mowbray to the Pennines

Wainwright's walk: St Bees to the Bay in forty hours non-stop. His legs collapsed around Kirkby Stephen, he did 30 miles of Swaledale on crutches, and by that time the other five had also wrecked their legs so they were finishing it in turns as a relay. Then back to work on Monday ....

Nothing refreshes like the suffering of others. I surge on strongly along the ironstone railway, wondering if it's possible to complete at least the Cleveland Hills tonight. Slow hillrunning can get you a surprisingly long way provided you do it for a very, very long time: and today did start at five.

The sun sank and shone out from under the grey, and what it shone onto was most deliciously bumpy. For here came another of Mr Wainwright's different bits. Here flat gives way to rumpled heather to bilberry and grass. And here, suddenly, are the Wainstones: a perfectly absurd set of gritstone pinnacles and blobs, perched on the edge of an abyss, with a long and fading view across the Vale of York. Some obliging rockclimbers posed for my camera on the grit blobs.

The evening stretched on. The rockclimbers climbed into their car, the last in the carpark. I ran alone along the stone pavement beside the green abyss. The track dropped off, clung to the skirts of the hillslope through various woods where the nettles were just coming up. I did

below: The moors above Swaledale are a mixture of fertile green and gritstone grey, with remains of ancient industry in interesting decay. This is the Surrender smelt mill above Reeth

not stop and sleep among the nettles, for there was still an hour left of light, and see! the way ascends again onto a last hill.

In summer this is nowhere special between a wall and a wood. On a spring evening, though, the wood is leafless, and beyond and through it – for it's a wood that drops suddenly – is the plain all twinkling with the headlamps of the A19 and various industrial cities. I'm peering through the bare twigs at Civilisation. I can see it but it can't see me ....

Civilisation is not so easily escaped. Orange lights shine on the branches, there are strident shapes of metal girderwork against the sky. Civilisation leaps out from behind a birch tree. It's the TV booster station built with minimal intrusion that man may speak microwaves to man across the North York Moors.

above: Swinner Gill. Natural erosion and the ravages of lead-mining combine to make spectacular scenery on the approach to Keld

The first range of foothills has been successfully penetrated – the second, higher, range blocks the horizon. But before it lies a wide flat plain. Our enemies here will be heat, and thirst – for the next drinkable stream is in those hills ahead. There's just one good way across the Vale of Mowbray, and that way is: as quickly as possible. A boring morning is one more example of the incredible variety of Mr Wainwright's walk. Actually, springtime is the good time: not just because of the burgeoning ploughland, the penetrating fragrance of the new-laid fertiliser or the merry tweeting of the muck-spreaders. In springtime, the grass grows over the field paths, offering fascinating navigation. It's as interesting as a misted hilltop, with the bonus of mud, ditches, and prickly hedges for when you go wrong. I get lost four times in as many miles – something you'd never manage on the Hartsop Car Park route up Kidsty Pike, or the well-trodden trek to Everest Base Camp.

Here in England we don't have to worry about the start of the Monsoon Season – it never stops. Swaledale is grey-green in the rain. Again the navigation is interesting, among high stone walls, following an optimistic signpost towards a stile beyond the brow of the hill. But now the surroundings are also interesting. The rain drips in the most dismal way off ancient yews and long angular crags, encouraging thoughts of blisters and early death. I press on through Reeth, giving the rain every chance to stop if it should be that way inclined .... Long slow hillrunning means not carrying heavy luxuries like dry clothes for the night, and if I go to bed wet, the bag's not going to dry out the rest of the way. Of course, lightweight polyester is just as warm when it's wet, but it does weigh more.

The rain, obligingly, stops coming down. I run on to dry out and let it get properly dark, and lie down at the rim of the moor. Slowly grey fades to black. Behind the heather the grouse let out occasional quacks; in front, in the fields, the odd sudden shriek of a pheasant. Thus lulled, sleep comes easily – you don't need a foam mat if you go far enough during the day.

The third day is more moor. Odd how the mist lies across the hillside, almost as if there were

snow up there. The track gets more remote, and higher – and that stuff that looks like snow is, indeed, snow. An abandoned stone-crusher stands at the moor-top, its windward side plastered with fresh slush. The way is not apparent: of the 10,000 people who walk to Kidsty Pike, not one has been kind enough to go ahead of me making footprints. Why aren't we going up green Swaledale anyway, Swaledale with the hanging woods and the gorge of limestone?

Gunnerside Gill: that's why not. We drop over an edge onto steep scree and crag, all man-made to uncover the lead ores underneath. Here are high rocks and ruins, narrow green tracks, and a river crossing made from a balanced slab. If this footbridge collapses under you, you'll be joined in the waterfall by a ton and a half of gritstone. Up-valley are more waterfalls, and a steep and slimy path to climb up out on. And after Gunnerside, Swinner: another vee-notch hollow, with a path slithering down to elegant stone arches and escaping across the steep side.

But already it's time for a different bit. After the slippery limestone mud above Keld comes the contrasting slippery peat mud of Nine Standards Rigg. The nine (actually ten) cairns huddle together for warmth, looking particularly sorry for themselves with snow drifting around their toes and a wraparound view of thick grey. A few ragged prayer flags might help here. Down below,

above: At 2171ft (662m), the ten cairns of Nine Standards Rigg mark the watershed of England

left: Kidsty Pike (780m), whose summit must be considered the most arduous in England. The most usual way up it involves five days of travel, a tent, and nearly 8000m of ascent

overleaf: Arrive at Lakeland fit and with good feet, and go wild – dashing off in all directions, but more particularly upwards. This diversion over Helm Crag is an accepted alternative on Wainwright's route. Those with lively imaginations and legs to match will throw away the book and head out to the sea by way of Eskdale or Grasmoor or the Wastwater Screes

a more cheerful pair of cairns on a knobby bit celebrate the arrival of the Westmorland limestone.

Actually, there's slightly too much of this. Westmorland limestone is grassy and fast, and this can be demoralising for a decelerating hillrunner. The countryside is speckled with ancient remains, and guidebook writers find these remains extremely interesting because that's their job. The rest of us may not be all that bothered whether the lump in the field is archaeology or not. It's not entirely Wainwright's fault. Wainwright trespassed boldly over the limestone pavement, and his first edition gives instruction in the art of climbing limestone walls without knocking too much off them. The more recent route is on a road.

After Orton is the dry valley, where you gain an inkling of limestone country – it has that green grass bottom and the weird limestone boulders sticking out of the side. I headed for what the map described as a comfy wood in the vicinity of Robin Hood's Grave. The first star twinkled through twisted birch-twigs. I unrolled the bag on some nice looking moss and went to sleep.

I woke up again just as the second star twinkled through the twisted birch-twigs. Underneath the nice moss were some very nasty limestone boulders. The comfy wood was a fraud. However, it was now dark and I'd already taken my shoes off. Those who lug tents and cookers have various evening treats, but the lightweight bivvy-bagger has just one thing to enjoy at end of day and that's to be not wearing his shoes.

The boulders, better than any alarm-clock, helped me rise to a dawn start. The dawn was a grey one, with mist grazing the moor top and more mist lingering in the moor-bottoms.

THE SUMMIT PUSH

At Shap you first notice a little kink in the skyline: the summit is in sight! For England's principal 8000m peak it doesn't look all that large. No doubt it'll be bigger when we get to it. But to get to it involves a lot of limestone fields, and fields need full concentration. Kidsty disappears again behind a wall-end. Now, though, this is becoming mountain country …. At the bottom of a wet field is a packhorse bridge, and the stones of the bridge are grey Borrowdale Volcanic. And then I raise my eyes to seek the second stile, and I'm looking straight into Mardale.

In September 1950, after four days up the Khumbu Glacier, Eric Shipton and Ed Hillary reached 20,000ft on Pumori and looked east; and they saw the long deep Western Cwm, the valley that leads in easily under Everest to the very foot of the Lhotse Face. And they knew that it was going to go.

Mardale isn't the Western Cwm – Mardale points east not west, and lacks

left: Most interesting of all the four Lakeland passes is the crossing from Grasmere to Borrowdale. The path descends with some relief from the complicated col of Greenup Edge, and is seen here emerging below the overhanging Eagle Crag into Langstrath

crevasses. But the two valleys serve the same function: to suck you in quickly among the mountains. I speed up suddenly, and bark my shin quite badly on the second stile. A field-edge leads down to a gate, and through the gate is a river with seven different sorts of tree, grey mossy rocks and a waterfall. I've arrived.

Haweswater entertains with imaginative notice-boards: in my innocence I hadn't even thought of damaging stones on the reservoir bed, and while I'll take all reasonable precautions against green algal slime, it's hard to get scared by the dangers of drinking water.

But mostly, Haweswater entertains by being Lakeland at last. The scenery slides up sideways and folds in behind itself. Water sploshes everywhere and no longer needs to be bought at a shop. Brown bracken lies along the fellsides. And soon there should be some nice thumping uphills to relax on. Soon too, the final assault on high Kidsty Pike.

A walker approaches dangling the distinctive Wainwright map. Kidsty is apparently a 'total no-go area' – it's under snow.

I stop and think about things. Does my route involve slopes where a slip in the slush could send me hurtling down the hillside? It might if I were to descend to Hartsop, but down by Satura Crag it does not. What about getting lost? It's a straightforward compass-bearing up, and a wall and fence down. The snow's too slushy for skiers, so I shouldn't get run over. That just leaves frostbite, which is a serious risk for runners in wet snow. However, I have plastic bags as emergency socks. I can see no reason not to make the final assault on Kidsty.

So that's how I climbed Kidsty Pike (2606ft/868m) in three days in May.

THE DESCENT

Slush-running was fun along the ridge of High Street. Down to Boredale Hause was soft and boggy, but the last drop to Patterdale was harsh. I stopped at the phone box to warn my family I was still alive despite the snow.

Someone wanted to know if this man by the phone box was all right. Well, nothing worse than sore feet. I took it they were not wondering about my motivation and psyche …. They were wondering about camera-angles. They were filming *The Lakes*, and I was in it. It was to be strong stuff, for after the nine o'clock watershed, but I was to look natural, not look at the camera, and carry on with what I was doing. So I emptied my pockets into the litter bin, but decided that me doing my blisters might be too strong even for after nine o'clock.

I'd planned to finish the trip with a wide-ranging romp taking in the Back o' Skiddaw and Grasmoor. But while I enjoy Lakeland hills in thick mist, it'd be quite nice to finish this while the sleeping bag's still dry.

And also, in mist, Grisedale Pass is really rather grand. The crags run up into the cloud; the top's a notch that comes and goes behind the swirls. The vague blacknesses above must be impending precipices – certainly some very large boulders have fallen down out of there. I hear the tarn before I see it. The few yards of it that do appear could stretch away for ever. Small waves lap against the stones, damp walkers appear and head down into the valley. The mountain is mine, mine alone.

At Grasmere it was still only teatime. With Helm Crag it's the shape that matters, and shapes are just as good in evening grey, so I went onto Helm Crag. The shapes were wet and colourless, but the sunlight had managed to find the lake. I chose my bed on Gibson Knott with care. Out of the wind, view towards the daybreak, and soft mossy grass: I intended to enjoy this night out on the mountain. And enjoy it I did, for about twenty seconds before I fell asleep.

The pass between Grasmere and Borrowdale is a peculiarly satisfying one. Its line is natural, but not obvious. A long green valley in; a long green valley out; and between them, an oblique crossing of a high bogbowl, and a necessary col that at almost 2000ft is scarcely lower than the hills it passes between. I've slightly spoilt this concept by not entering along Far Easedale. (Helm Crag is fine, but so is Easedale with its stream, willow trees and waterfalls at the head.) However, I still get the full feeling of the green bogbowl. The head of Wythburn is circled by low hillocks; soggy grass below and sky above. Here dry socks, hot drinks and Civilisation itself are lost beyond the rim. The mist's well down and recent rainfall has filled up the bogs and overflowed what paths there are. Now, I may get lost in the fields of Swaledale, but I don't get lost in the hills … do I?

Of course I don't. Circle the head of the bog, watch the direction of the contours and find a pretty big path up the slope to Greenup Edge. The path down the back tries to run away, but it's easily pinned down with the needle of the compass. The long green valley out is Langstrath, which has a bottom of glaciated hummocks, and a splendid crag that actually overhangs, and a roof of grey cloud.

Ahead now lies Borrowdale, leading to Keswick and its urban lifestyle of cafés and mountain shops. The Wainwright Walk and I are not quite ready for this much Civilisation; so we turn sharply aside to Honister.

This last pass is less exciting, rising beside the road and then taking to stony paths. And the forest road of Ennerdale induces thoughts of the simple pleasures of no longer walking towards, or away from, Kidsty Pike – such pleasures as dry socks, a shave and a hot shower. I consult the timetable to see if it can make the final stage more interesting – and it can! To complete this in five days, it'll be necessary to reach St Bees by 8 o'clock tonight. And that means six hours for the final 20 miles (32km), and the 20 do have some hills in. In other words – slow running.

Do not consider why one should wish to reach St Bees in this time. A real running time is two days, not five. The eastbound Saturday Starters are coming towards me now, and they all want to know how long it's taken me. So I mumble: it's my preferred speed, I'm a runner so I sort of run some bits, and did they notice the rotated signpost on Dent Fell?

So, along the tracks and roads of West Cumbria, I occupied the brain with calculations and counting the miles, and the legs with trying to do those miles a bit faster. It worked: the hedges separated, the sea appeared, I was on the cliff-top finale. And I'd nearly two hours for the final 4 miles (6km), which would permit a contemplative slow-down, but the weather said none of that and sent a sharp cold rain to keep me on the move.

Rain hissed on grey concrete, the tide was out and St Bees was agreeably dismal in the evening light. I booked into a hotel, washed my clothes, washed myself, got back into the clothes and dried out in the bar. The following morning, the sun almost came out. I wandered back along the cliffs to take pictures of the birds. A man with a rucksack came up the steps from St Bees, just setting off on the long march in to Kidsty Pike.

I told him about the rotated signpost on Dent Fell.

overleaf: The crossing from Honister into Ennerdale is the walk's last hard ground. Honister's youth hostel offers this Buttermere sunset before a final night among the mountains

above: As well as plenty of mountain ground, Wainwright's walk has more than its fair share of woods and waterfalls. Kisdon Force is one of several that can be visited in an evening stroll out of Keld

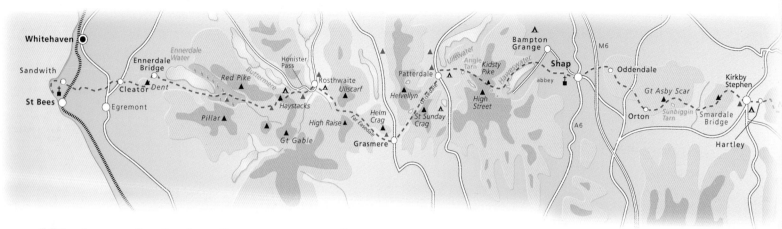

Wainwright's Coast-to-Coast: The Route

In the later chapters we'll give quite detailed notes on the exact routes. On Wainwright's Coast-to-Coast you have strip-maps by the OS and by Footprint, and a choice of four guidebooks. But if you do navigate it using only this description, you'll be doing just what Wainwright wanted. He always saw his route as a mere baseline around which we walkers should improvise our own variations.

Most walkers follow Wainwright and travel eastwards towards Yorkshire. The first reason, which is sound enough except in those years when it isn't, is to have the wind and weather behind. The second reason is to get the Lakeland tough bit over at the start. But it's better to keep the tough bit to the end, when you're fit. And though all the walk is good (except the Vale of Mowbray), the Lakeland bit is the best and should be saved till last. Arrive at Lakeland fit and with good feet, and go wild – dashing off in all directions to arrive at the sea by way of Eskdale or Grasmoor or the Wastwater Screes.

The walk falls into twelve sections, each quite different from the rest.

THE SEA AND ESKDALE
■ The first section is the closest Wainwright comes to a pretty bit. Even so, the honey is enclosed in slices of brown wholemeal, as a grim heather moor divides up the day.
■ The route follows high gritstone clifftops round to Hawsker. Greystones Hill is the first bleak moorland, but we quickly drop into the wooded hollow of

the May Beck and follow it down to Littlebeck. Little heather paths cross into Eskdale, and this pleasant valley is followed to Glaisdale.

NORTH YORK MOORS
■ Fast flat paths cross the high plateau. Ancient waymarks and peculiar standing stones do their best to lighten the atmosphere. Old unsurfaced roads lead up Glaisdale Rigg, then round the head of Great Fryup Dale, Danby Dale and Rosedale, to the welcome shelter of the Lion Inn with its gay orange pantiles. The flinty track of the ironstone railway leads to Bloworth Crossing.

CLEVELAND HILLS
■ This is a section of small but surprising hills, steep-sided and with rocky outcrops and crags. You go up and down, up and down, over Hasty Bank and Cringle Moor, Carlton Bank and Beacon Hill, and all the time on the right is a huge and hazy view of the Vale of York and industrial Middlesbrough.
■ Just before Osmotherley the way doubles back through Arncliffe Wood and drops off the edge to Ingleby Cross.

VALE OF MOWBRAY
■ Flat ground of field edges and farm tracks leads by way of Sydal Lodge, Wray House and Lovesome Hill to Danby Wiske. It's a good plan to spend the night at Danby Wiske, so as to have the unexciting Vale of Mowbray as two half-days rather than one whole one.
■ You can take the roads via Streetlam, which is quicker, or the field paths by

Kiplin Hall, which is slightly more stimulating but gets your legs wet.
■ Things improve at Ellerton Hill, where you pick up a small beck. From Catterick the Swale leads up to stone-built Richmond with its castle and market.

SWALEDALE
■ How satisfying it is to follow a river all the way. Swaledale is green and busy in its lower stretches, but after Reeth the moor starts to close in. The route then leaves Swaledale for something more interesting: the ravaged ground of the lead mines. Steep and sudden are the drops into Gunnerside Gill and Swinner Gill.
■ In its sheltered hollow at the head of the Swale, Keld is the crossing of Wainwright's Coast-to-Coast and the Pennine Way. In walking terms, this is the intersection of all England.

NINE STANDARDS RIGG
■ The crossing from Keld to Kirkby Stephen is where Wainwright's route shows you the peat bog and makes you happy you didn't do the Pennine Way instead. On a sunny spring day the meadow pipits twitter and there's a view (they say) to the North Sea and Atlantic. The rest of the time the black slime rises up your gaiters and there's a view of bog cotton.
■ There are different permissive paths over Nine Standards for different times of the year, with a winter route round the side on public footpaths.

WESTMORLAND LIMESTONE
■ The long green tracks of the limestone

country are dry underfoot and make for fast travel. This is pleasant for its contrast with Nine Standards; pleasant also for the forgotten hollow of Smardale Bridge, and (after Orton) the little bit of limestone pavement on Crosby Ravensworth Fell. A brief ugly moment with Hardendale Quarry, the M6 and the cement factory is there just to heighten your enjoyment of the Lake District ahead.

SHAP TO PATTERDALE
■ The crossing of Lakeland involves four passes, which are quite unalike. After a walk in along the Haweswater Reservoir, the route crosses the felltops, over Kidsty Pike and round the flank of the Knott. It's high and exposed for a considerable distance, and a tough introduction to the real hill ground.

GRISEDALE HAUSE
■ This is a classic pass: a long sheltered valley in, and then a high notch between crags. Grisedale Tarn nestles below the pass but above the rest of the world.

GRASMERE TO BORROWDALE
■ The third pass is particularly satisfying. The charming dead-end valley of Far Easedale leads to a complicated crossing: there are two separate cols and a boggy place between where you feel lost even if you aren't. (Quite often you are!) Once found, the way down drops into another dead-end valley. Greenup has high overhanging crags and oakwoods and a stony path to the prettiest place in England.

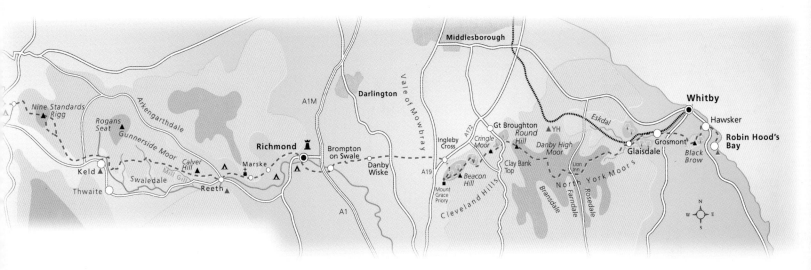

HONISTER & ENNERDALE

■ The final pass lets you out more easily. The old road gives lingering views of Borrowdale, and the crossing by the Honister quarries to Ennerdale is a matter of going up the tramway and down the stony gill.

■ Forestry plantations do not improve Ennerdale, but by crossing the river immediately under Pillar Rock you can find a riverside footpath. The walk along the southern shore of Ennerdale Water is a fine way out of Lakeland.

CUMBRIA COASTAL

■ The last day starts well. After Ennerdale Bridge, the route drops into the glacier meltwater channel of Nannycatch and climbs out over Dent hill.

■ Less interesting tracks and field paths lead by Cleator and Moor Row to Sandwith. The final clifftop path around to St Bees is very fine.

ESSENTIAL INFORMATION

Start: Robin Hood's Bay, North Yorkshire
Finish: St Bees, Cumbria
Distance: 190 miles (300km)
Distance on roads: between 40 miles (64km) and 20 miles (32km) depending on route chosen
Total ascent: 25,000ft (7500m)
Time: 14 days (of 14mls/22km) suits most walkers and keeps you in step with the luggage-ahead services
Terrain: Very varied, with valley, moorland, lakeside, field and mountain. Short stretches of steep or boggy ground in Lakeland and the Pennines, but mostly moderate or easy walking on clear paths

MAPS AND GUIDES

OS Outdoor Leisure 34 and 33 – the Coast-to-Coast strip maps. Those adventuring off-route will supplement with Outdoor Leisure 27, 26, 30, 19, 5 and 4. Map of alternative routes over Nine Standards (free from Kirkby Stephen TI)
Coast to Coast by Ronald Turnbull (Dalesman) includes compressed East-to-West description. No full-length East-West guidebook exists
Coast to Coast B&B Guide from Mrs D. Whitehead, Butt House, Keld, Richmond D11 6LJ
Website: www.coast2coast.co.uk

TRANSPORT

The start and finish are served by stations, though it's quicker to reach Robin Hood's Bay by bus from Middlesbrough or Scarborough. There is a station at Kirkby Stephen, and Grasmere has express coaches. Buses link most points on the walk with Whitehaven, Penrith, Kirkby Stephen, Darlington and Whitby. Cumbria travel information on 01228 606000, and free timetables for Cumbria, Yorkshire Dales, North York Moors from local TI Centres

TOURIST INFORMATION

Whitehaven 01946 695678
Grasmere 01539 435245
Kirkby Stephen 01768 371199
Richmond 01748 850252
Whitby 01947 602674

Key to Maps

- - - Main route

.... alternative route

▲ youth hostel

Λ campsite

▲ mountain/hill top

✝ church or abbey

♜ Castle

🌲 forest or wood

DISTANCE CHART (cumulative)

	MLS	KM	COMMENTS
Robin Hood's Bay	0	0	
Hawsker	4	6	no shop
Littlebeck	12	19	B&B only
Grosmont	16	26	
Egton Bridge	18	29	no shop
Glaisdale	21	34	
Lion Inn	31	50	inn only
(Great Broughton + 2mls)			
Green Bank	43	69	café only
Ingleby Cross	53	85	
Lovesome Hill	61	98	bunkhouse only
Danby Wiske	63	101	no shop
Bolton-on-Swale	70	113	
Catterick Bridge	72	116	
Colburn	74	119	
Richmond	76	122	
Applegarth	80	128	bunkhouse only
Marske	82	132	no shop
Marrick	84	135	no shop

	MLS	KM	COMMENTS
Reeth	88	142	YH Grinton
Keld	94	151	YH
Kirkby Stephen	109	175	YH
Bents Farm	115	185	bunkhouse, B&B only
Orton	122	196	
Shap	129	208	bunkhouse
Patterdale	145	233	YH
Grasmere	153	246	YH
Rosthwaite	162	261	bunkhouse, YH
Seatoller	163	262	no shop
Honister Hause	165	265	YH only
Black Sail	167	269	YH only
Gillerthwaite	172	277	YH only
Ennerdale Bridge	177	285	
Cleator	181	291	
Moor Row	182	293	
Sandwith	187	301	
St Bees	191	307	

Bristol Channel to Irish Sea

Offa's Dyke

The Border Lines

above: The magnificent arches of Tintern Abbey

right: The official Offa's Dyke Path bypasses Tintern, choosing instead to look at it through the trees of the high valleysides. However, most walkers make a detour to see the impressive twelfth-century Cistercian abbey

U nder Saxon rule, Wales had no need for political borders, for Wales had hills: the English border kingdoms, in general, did not. So the foothills seemed to satisfy the early warlords until Offa. This Saxon king had extended his Mercian borders as far as Northumberland and Wessex, and had other ideas. The Welsh were not a major threat, just a nuisance. Offa needed to flex his muscles. He decided on a border dyke. Maybe it would not be in the class of Hadrian's Wall, but Hadrian was Roman, and had more soldiers and slaves to build it for him. Offa's wall would be symbolic rather than strategic.

Little did Offa know that in trying to keep the Welsh out of Mercia he would centuries later entice new armies over his earthworks. Twentieth-century walkers liked the idea of the Dyke for company: after all, this was a coast-to-coast earthwork, passing through some darned good countryside, and there were castles, old Iron Age forts and lovely valleys *en route*.

At first Offa's Dyke seeks the shade of the Wye Valley woodlands. Then there's the first of many gaps – from Redbrook right through to Kington, covering much of the Herefordshire sandstone area. The mystery of this bit of missing dyke was solved by Sir Cyril Fox, who discovered that in Offa's day the place was blanketed by impenetrable forest. Here, the path heads for high ground – the Black Mountains.

From Kington to the Ceiriog Valley near Chirk, Offa's Dyke is at its best. Even when confronted by the chaotic east–west ridges of the Clun Forest it runs powerfully up and down the hillsides without wavering. In Flintshire the Dyke runs through what was coal-mining country, and sensibly the path leaves it for the heathery Clwydian Hills.

It has to be said that Offa designed a mighty fine path.

MUD AND GUTS

So here were Nicola and I on a sunny Saturday afternoon in late April, following the Offa's Dyke Path through the woods north of Chepstow. Down through the trees, the sleepy Wye meandered among fields that were green after weeks of rain. Four miles ahead at Tintern was our first night's B&B.

Our walk had started a few miles back in Chepstow, a busy little town where the Wye, brown with tidal mud, flowed swiftly by the ramparts of a powerful castle. Attractive streets of shops offered last chances to stock up with the things that had been forgotten the night before – another pair of socks for me; a couple of Mars bars for Nicola.

Tintern Abbey appeared through the trees; tantalisingly close, but in reality, still a mile or two away. The B&B was a pretty cottage next to the Cistercian abbey and right by the riverbank. And, inside there was a cup of tea waiting for us – this was all very civilised.

Next morning the sun had gone. 'Two or three days of rain,' the weatherman informed us. After managing the first of many breakfasts of bacon, egg and sausage we went out into the rain, clad in our pristine waterproofs. Past Bigsweir we climbed through more woodland where oak, beech, holly and lime perched high on the valley sides above the Wye. The river was still brown with mud. So now were the woodland paths, but the scent of bluebells and wild garlic was a heady mix, and the trees gave us a certain amount of shelter. Across the valley the dark steaming forests, some conifer and some oak, were punctuated by little clearings with huddled whitewashed houses and the odd riverside inn.

After making us come down to the valley at Redbrook, the Offa's Dyke Path wanted us to go back up the hill to Kymin. Offa's reward was a naval temple and an airy view of Monmouth. We were having none of this, for the Wye Valley Walk offered us an easy riverbank way into Monmouth.

We didn't give historic Monmouth the time it deserved, for we still had 4 miles before nightfall, 3 of them uphill. Statues of Henry V and C S Rolls of Rolls-Royce fame watched over us as we hurried past Agincourt Square and through a little ginnel with antique shops. Giving the fine thirteenth-century gatehouse of Monnow Bridge a cursory glance, we headed up a road fittingly called Watery Lane. The map told us the last hill of the day was called Long Hill. The forestry track up it seemed to go on and on – longer even than that name had promised – but the last mile to our B&B at Hendre Farm was easy and downhill.

above: Spring makes the woodlands of the Wye colourful with wildflowers, but it can also add a bit of a squelch to your walk. Here you see Quicken Tree Wood near Bigsweir

right: Looking up at Hay Bluff from Hay Common. It's the last of the Black Mountains visited by Offa's Dyke. When you're standing on the summit, you've left the horrible peat bogs behind

The third day was a transitional one. After the lovely Wye Valley, the rolling farmland seemed a little bit tame. The rain rained, and the mud still flowed. It was good red mud that lodged itself in every cleat of our bootsoles. I'd hoped for a newsagent at Llantilio Crossenny. There wasn't one: just a church, attractive through it was, and a pub, The Hostry. It was early for a pint, and a bit late for salvation, so we pressed on, over rolling pastures, with the ghostly grey outlines of distant peaks peeping over the hedges.

I hadn't expected much of White Castle, but it turned out to be rather splendid and, better still, free. It's not white; the whitewash has long since been removed. However, there's an impressive moat round the inner walls and a well-preserved keep.

The Black Mountains appeared through the damp grey atmosphere – not the proud, rock-fringed escarpment we had anticipated, but a faded shadow, capped with wispy clag.

The sound of rustling waterproofs and fast-moving bootsteps made us look back up the hill. Two walkers were moving just as swiftly as the rustling had suggested.

Jenny and Josh were doing Land's End to John O'Groats. Offa's Dyke was a short link in their itinerary. We picked up speed and walked with them down to Pandy.

Some places look unpromising and the Lancaster Arms in Pandy was one of them – just a turn-of-the-century box of a building between two roads – but it gave us one of our most enjoyable nights of the walk. Here we shared the company of people whom we were to meet and remeet along the whole of the route.

Next morning the cloud hung even lower across the green foothills of the Hatterrall ridge. Having done the Black Mountains before, I knew that their valleys were much nicer than their ridges. The tops reminded me of the worst of parts of the Peak and Pennines. We planned a route through the Olchon Valley before climbing the narrow rocky ridge to Black Hill, then onwards to the main ridge near Hay Bluff. 'Where are you off to, then?' asked a man on the street by Longtown Castle. 'Black Hill.' 'We pulled a bloke out from there last Thursday. It's just a mire.' The man was from the local mountain rescue team and told us about a bridleway that goes round the mountain and onto Hay Common.

This route was pretty. The lanes had sweet-smelling hedgerows with flower-filled verges, and we could see the odd spot of sun highlighting distant hillsides. Bathed in sunlight and standing proud above the common, Hay Bluff looked impressive. The path up it was steep, but we were compelled to make amends for having such an easy day by climbing to the top.

At Hay, we had a B&B, aptly named 'Rest for the Tired', and ate a bar meal at Kilverts, one of the best pubs for food in Wales. Kilverts was heaving with hungry hillwalkers, bookbuyers and locals.

OVER THE GREEN HILLS OF RADNOR

The Wye is one of Britain's loveliest rivers, and this morning it was bathed in sunshine and flecked with wildflowers. My camera battery decided this beauty was too much for it to take in, gave me one picture, then died.

left: Offa's Dyke takes you across many long, grassy ridges. Here at Hawthorn Hill above Kington, you are looking down to the Lugg Valley

Once out of the valley, Offa's Dyke threads through devious countryside of small hills and remote farming valleys. It uses the odd country lane and wanders through wooded dingles. I remember seeing apple blossom in abundance and hearing dogs and shepherds on distant pastures. The high point of the day was to be Hergest Ridge. Being a bit of a Mike Oldfield fan I had bought the record. Now I needed to climb the hill.

Today, Hergest Ridge was not at its best, for the views from this free-striding grass and bracken ridge were lost in a dull, grey mist. Sinister silhouettes appeared through this mist. Hergest is known for its mysteries – the Whet Stone, for instance, goes down the hill each morning for a drink of water. As we neared the sinister silhouettes, they cleverly turned themselves into Monkey Puzzle trees   perhaps under the spell of the local ghost, Black Vaughan, or his murderous wife; or maybe they were an evil experiment in genetic engineering.

Kington greeted us with an attractive spired church, half hidden by the blossom of cherry trees. On Offa's Dyke you cross the border that many times you're seldom sure whether you're in England or Wales. At Kington there's no doubt: it's a typically English market town, with a market square with pubs, a High Street of Georgian and Victorian shops and a pretty river running through it.

Next day, after crossing dew-soaked fields by the River Arrow, we climbed back to Offa's Dyke proper at Rushock Hill. The path gets more erratic in its quest to seek out the elusive dyke. After dropping down to the wide green valley of Hindwell Brook and climbing past the delightfully restored half-timbered farmhouse of Burfa, the path finds the Dyke more helpful and stays with it across the high pastures of Hawthorn Hill to Knighton where we stayed the night.

The book said this was to be the toughest section of the route. It calls these next hills the Switchbacks, though the map calls them the Clun Hills. As we strode the flat high sections of Llanfair Hill, we wondered what the fuss was about. This was a grand pastured ridge with the dyke, now straight and proud, for company, and with one wonderful section in the shade of some larch trees. But Llanfair Hill and the dyke finally deposit you back on the roadside, and the road goes downhill to another path, which takes you further down – in fact, to the very bottom of – the Clun Valley.

Now the Clun Valley goes east and Offa wanted his dyke to go north. So back up the hill you go, then round into an anonymous, twisting cwm that makes you climb towards another steep-sided spur, Hergan. The path has you crossing a series of pastured spurs to Knuck Bank. Here, you have hit the heights. But the path dumps you into depths of despair by diving straight down into Cwm Ffrydd.

We studied the view for some time.

'Lovely place. We must come back here sometime … without these heavy packs.'

Churchtown, at the bottom of Cwm Ffrydd, has the church, but not the town. The climb away from it

below: The Offa's Dyke Path is at its best on high ridges where you walk the line of the dyke itself. Here, on the approach to Llanfair Hill, the walker is also offered the shade of larch trees

was steep, and my trainers only just gripped the grassy hillside. It's now all downhill to our B&B at Little Brompton Farm.

above: Chirk Castle seen through a spring morning haze. Beyond Chirk the path sees little of the real Dyke

ACROSS THE SHROPSHIRE FLATLANDS – BROMPTON CROSSROADS TO SELATTYN

They call this next stage the flat bit. Well, we were due a bit of a rest. I got lost looking for Offa's Dyke at the back of the farm. Half an hour later we were back on course and really motoring. After lunch at the pub at Forden, we had one 'up', the Long Mountain, to do before a long flat section through the Severn Valley. Beacon Ring, at the top of the mountain, had looked promising, but, disappointingly, it turned out to be obscured by forest.

'There's a view from the crags of Llanymynech Hill,' the book proclaimed – not on this day, though. There were some limestone quarried crags to explore, and another golf course to negotiate before coming down the other side of the hill in the company of thousands of mayflies. This was to be a long day, but a good one, with the afternoon sun filtering through a thick haze that would have drawn Turner back to his canvas.

THE HOME RUN – SELATTYN TO PRESTATYN

The stretch from Selattyn to the Dee is the last you see of the Dyke itself, and it's fitting that the earthworks are prominent and substantial. You're soon looking down on the beautiful Ceiriog valley and across to the imposing Chirk Castle.

Getting back up the other side of the valley to the castle was made easier by the woodland's shade. Cars lined the lane by the outer walls. This was going to be a bumper bank holiday weekend for the National Trust.

From the castle we dropped down the hillside to join the Llangollen canal. The canal is high up on the south side of the valley and has to cross to the north; hence Telford's masterpiece, the Pont Cysyllte aqueduct. Here, a cast iron trough carries the canal for a kilometre, 120ft (36m) above the River Dee. Queues of people and a couple of colourful barges were crossing it. On the other side at Trefor, scores more were sitting on the grass, eating ice creams.

Though most Offa's Dykers do Llangollen, it's 2 miles off the route. Llangollen Bridge is a nice one. You can while away time, hanging over the edge looking at the trout swimming in the fast-flowing Dee. Today, revellers were diving into the river to join the fish.

The next morning Llangollen itself had a hangover: the bank holiday was gone and the place was silent as we set off in search of World's End. The castle on the conical hill, Dinas Bran, watched from on high as we rounded its lower slopes to rejoin the Offa's Dyke route.

right: Eglwyseg Crags form part of a long line of tiered limestone running between Llangollen and World's End. Offa's Dyke first follows country lanes beneath the escarpment, then continues on exciting scree paths at the foot of the cliffs

To get to World's End you walk on scree paths beneath the fine limestone cliffs of Eglwyseg. This is one of the walk's highlights. But World's End is not much of a place for such a grand name – a car park, two limestone crags peeping out from a conifer-filled hollow, and lots of confused motorists driving up and down the road looking for the real World's End.

Beyond World's End, the limestone terrain gives way to peaty heather moorland, and I felt I was back on the Pennines. There was just a bit of field-walking, then a few Clwydian outliers to be done before tea, and our B&B.

Our B&B at Clwyd Gate turned out to be a sixteenth-century farmhouse with tiny windows and original beamed ceilings that pub landlords would pay a king's ransom for. Mrs Gates ran an old-fashioned B&B – no *en suite* rooms, no separate guests' dining room, no television and no weather forecasts. But Mrs Gates did us all a b-i-g breakfast. It fuelled us for the ups and downs of the Clwydian range, and her for the canvassing she was about to do for the first Welsh Parliament elections.

By ten we were standing on the biggest peak, Moel Fammau. Last time we were here we had to share the old fort on top with well over a hundred walkers. This time there were only four others. One of the advantages of long-distance walking is that you get to see such places when everybody else is at work.

You can see the whole of Snowdonia from Moel Fammau, but not in today's haze. We moved on through the heather to see the Iron Age fort on Moel Arthur, a steep climb, and then the even bigger fort on Moel Penycloddiau.

THE LAST DAY

The last day was a bit of an anticlimax. Its first hill may have been little, but it was steep, and the path seemed to go to great lengths not to avoid its steepest slopes. We advanced onto the last of the book's maps by lunchtime and the Prestatyn cliffs an hour later. Prestatyn town sprawled across a narrow coastal plain, but the sea was still disguising itself as part of the sky.

A long, straight lane descended from the bottom of the hill into Prestatyn and turned into the high street. Past the newsagents, the souvenir shops and the cafés we went 'til we reached the end of the road. Prestatyn's concrete sea-defence walls were a strange and unfitting end to the walk. Perhaps we should have waited until the tide went out. It is a tradition for the Offa's Dyker to continue the line of the path out to sea for as far as he or she dares! Well, we didn't have bathing costumes and the sea looked quite boisterous and freezing. Instead, we settled for signing the Offa's Dyke book in the Tourist Information Office.

Somewhere under the tarmac and unnoticed, Offa's Dyke, having made its way through the suburbs of Prestatyn, flopped wearily into the sea.

Offa's Dyke: The Route

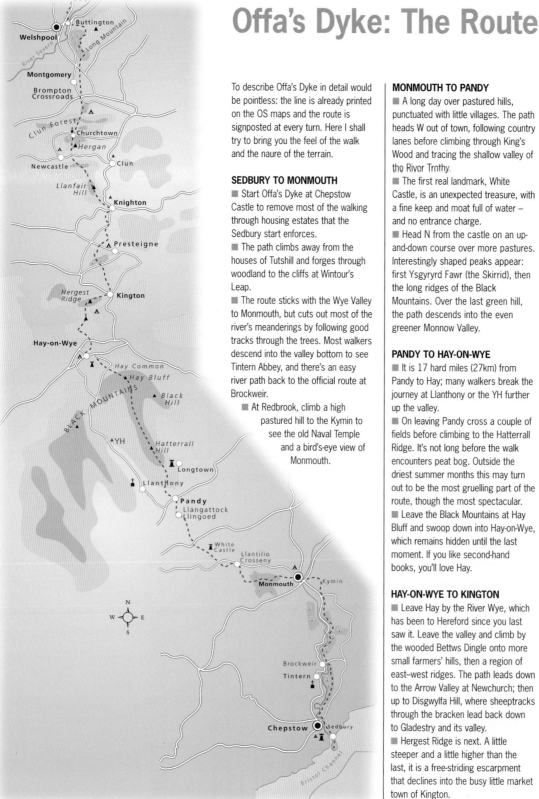

To describe Offa's Dyke in detail would be pointless: the line is already printed on the OS maps and the route is signposted at every turn. Here I shall try to bring you the feel of the walk and the naure of the terrain.

SEDBURY TO MONMOUTH

■ Start Offa's Dyke at Chepstow Castle to remove most of the walking through housing estates that the Sedbury start enforces.

■ The path climbs away from the houses of Tutshill and forges through woodland to the cliffs at Wintour's Leap.

■ The route sticks with the Wye Valley to Monmouth, but cuts out most of the river's meanderings by following good tracks through the trees. Most walkers descend into the valley bottom to see Tintern Abbey, and there's an easy river path back to the official route at Brockweir.

■ At Redbrook, climb a high pastured hill to the Kymin to see the old Naval Temple and a bird's-eye view of Monmouth.

MONMOUTH TO PANDY

■ A long day over pastured hills, punctuated with little villages. The path heads W out of town, following country lanes before climbing through King's Wood and tracing the shallow valley of the River Trothy.

■ The first real landmark, White Castle, is an unexpected treasure, with a fine keep and moat full of water – and no entrance charge.

■ Head N from the castle on an up-and-down course over more pastures. Interestingly shaped peaks appear: first Ysgyryrd Fawr (the Skirrid), then the long ridges of the Black Mountains. Over the last green hill, the path descends into the even greener Monnow Valley.

PANDY TO HAY-ON-WYE

■ It is 17 hard miles (27km) from Pandy to Hay; many walkers break the journey at Llanthony or the YH further up the valley.

■ On leaving Pandy cross a couple of fields before climbing to the Hatterrall Ridge. It's not long before the walk encounters peat bog. Outside the driest summer months this may turn out to be the most gruelling part of the route, though the most spectacular.

■ Leave the Black Mountains at Hay Bluff and swoop down into Hay-on-Wye, which remains hidden until the last moment. If you like second-hand books, you'll love Hay.

HAY-ON-WYE TO KINGTON

■ Leave Hay by the River Wye, which has been to Hereford since you last saw it. Leave the valley and climb by the wooded Bettws Dingle onto more small farmers' hills, then a region of east–west ridges. The path leads down to the Arrow Valley at Newchurch; then up to Disgwylfa Hill, where sheeptracks through the bracken lead back down to Gladestry and its valley.

■ Hergest Ridge is next. A little steeper and a little higher than the last, it is a free-striding escarpment that declines into the busy little market town of Kington.

KINGTON TO KNIGHTON

■ A steep path climbs past the golf course at Bradnor Green and onto Rushock Hill, where the path reacquaints itself with the Dyke proper. Again the hills are unhelpfully stretched across the route, and the path makes devious detours round the sides of steep slopes and into the valley of Hindwell Brook.

■ After climbing Evenjobb Hill past a magnificent half-timbered farmhouse, Burfa, descend to the beautiful Lugg Valley at Dolly Green. Then climb to an airy ridge on Hawthorn Hill, where the Dyke runs triumphantly over the tops before descending into Knighton.

KNIGHTON TO MONTGOMERY

■ The best section of the walk, although one of the toughest. After a short stroll by the river, climb the very steep slopes of Panpunton Hill, where there's a marvellous view down the Teme Valley.

■ After an easy time strolling the grassy ridges of Llanfair Hill, the path and the Dyke hurtle into the Clun Valley.

■ The next section is known as the Switchbacks and is why today's walk is a hard one. There's no real order to these hills and they lead the path a merry dance. It tries to take an orderly route by climbing round the sides of Graig Hill, descending into a deep and narrow valley, before climbing to a high road on Hergan (hill). Then it makes a beeline north.

■ Offa's route descends to the Unk Valley before making the day's last climb. On the top it crosses the Kerry Ridgeway, a famous old drove road, now under tarmac. From here it descends into the flatlands of Brompton, passing through the grounds of Mellington Hall (campsite) and on to Brompton Crossroads (B&B). More field paths along the Dyke bring the route to within striking distance of Montgomery, a wonderful old county town tucked beneath a hilltop castle.

MONTGOMERY TO LLANYMYNECH

■ The next stages are relatively flat, but they start with the Long Mountain just beyond Forden. The route starts on tarmac, but soon diverts left through the forest to reach the ancient Beacon Ring fort, which, disappointingly, is fenced off. Instead of continuing along the impressive-looking Breidden Hills, the route opts for a low-level line though the Severn Valley. At Buttington it uses the canal towpath, then follows the banks of the Severn, which leads into Four Crosses village.

■ To save a mile of A-road walking, the OD path turns left down Parsons Lane and follows the canal towpath for 2 miles (3km) into Llanymynech.

LLANYMYNECH TO THE CEIRIOG VALLEY (CHIRK)

■ The path takes to the hills again. Llanymynech Hill has been heavily quarried and has a golf course on top, but it's an interesting hill with wide views across the Severn plains.

■ The next hill, Moelydd Uchaf, has a flagpole on it and even better views, including the Berwyn and Aran ranges and the Long Mynd. Back down there's more field walking, a pub for lunch at Trefonen or, if you're fast, at Tyn y Coed in the Candy Valley.

■ Climb through Candy Woods and you're back following the Dyke proper, though the path diverts for a short while past the old racecourse. It's a fine section of the Dyke, too, and leads you safely across the hilltops and down to Bronygarth in the beautiful Ceiriog Valley.

Key to Maps

- – ᐧ ᐧ – Main route

----------- alternative route

▲ youth hostel

Δ campsite

▲ mountain/hill top

♰ church or abbey

♟ Castle

forest or wood

THE CEIRIOG VALLEY (CHIRK) TO LLANDEGLA

■ Since Mount Wood, the great sandstone castle of Chirk has been peeping across the valley from its high woodland setting. The path climbs though the castle's parklands and past its ornamental gates.

■ After following country lanes over the hilltops, descend high meadows into the Vale of Llangollen to follow the canal towpath.

■ At Pont Cysyllte a huge aqueduct carries you and the canal to the other side of the valley at Trefor. Trefor's an industrial town, and the path turns away to follow a panoramic walk on a limestone escarpment with fine views across to Castell Dinas Bran, a ruined hilltop castle.

■ Paths and a country lane continue beneath Craig Eglwyseg to reach World's End, a rather grandiose name for a car park in a spruce wood.

■ After a stiff climb up a tarmac road there's a duckboard traverse of peaty heather moorland, followed by forestry tracks through more conifers to reach Llandegla.

LLANDEGLA TO BODFARI

■ Another big day, taking in most of the Clwydian ridge. It starts with a complex traverse of farm fields, then takes to the foothills with Moel y Plas. At first the route skirts the hilltops, but it does so on good paths with lovely views across the chequered plains of the Vale of Clwyd.

■ Beyond the busy A494 at Clwyd Gate the hills get higher. There's a splendid promenade on a green track through heather and bilberry slopes. Climb to the earthworks of Foel Fenlli's fort, then continue on wide flinted Landrover tracks to the Jubilee Tower capping Moel Fammau. This is the highest point of the Clwydians.

■ The next few miles is all good ridge walking over heathered hills, with a steep descent and reascent to the fort on Moel Arthur. The OD path comes down to the valley, following attractive farm tracks into Bodfari.

BODFARI TO PRESTATYN

■ You've done all the best bits now, whatever the guide books tell you. But this day is a relatively easy one, and that's nice at the end of a walk. The climb out of Bodfari is short but steep. The Clwydians are smaller hills now, in height and in girth. OD is now a series of country lanes and field paths.

■ Beyond Rhuallt the route makes long meanderings to avoid the forestry of Mynydd Y Cwm. You will be tempted to follow one of the roads to save time.

■ On Marian Ffrith the sea comes into view between two craggy hills. There are more field paths to be done, but soon you are walking that final couple of miles along the last escarpment, and looking down upon Prestatyn. The last mile is along the main street. The seashore is a little different to Sedbury Cliffs: it's imprisoned by concrete walls. If the tide's in you may feel let down. Tradition says that if it's out, you have to keep walking across the sands to the water's edge. This would provide a more satisfactory finish to what is one of the best long-distance walks in the UK.

ESSENTIAL INFORMATION

Start: Sedbury Cliffs, Chepstow
Finish: Prestatyn
Distance: 174 miles (280km)
Total Ascent: 45,000ft (15,000m)
Time: 10–14 days
Terrain: Varied. Much of the early walk is through woodland and pasture. The Black Mountain is on high and serious mountain ground (very marshy at times). Though the rest of the walk isn't as high-level as Snowdonia to Gower, there are a lot of ups and downs

MAPS AND GUIDES

OS Landranger 1:50 000 Nos 172, 161, 162, 148, 137, 125, 117, 116
Offa's Dyke North and *Offa's Dyke South* (2 volumes) by Ernie and Kathy Kay, and Mark Richards (Aurum Press). The most useful book and one with all the maps (OS 1:25 000) you'll need

above: On the towpath of the Llangollen Canal
right: Moel Eithinen, one of the Clwydian outliers

TRANSPORT
Rail: Prestatyn is on the North Wales Coast line with trains from Chester. Chepstow has trains linking it with Birmingham, Worcester and Gloucester. Buses: National Express run buses from London, Birmingham and Chester to Prestatyn. They also have services from Birmingham to Monmouth (for Chepstow), and Swansea to Gatwick, calling at Chepstow

TOURIST INFORMATION
The main year-round tourist offices are:
Chepstow: 01291 623772
Brecon (for Hay area)
01874 622485
Knighton 01547 528753
Welshpool 01938 552043
Llangolle: 01978 860828
Rhyl (for Prestatyn area
01745 355068

Addresses
Offa's Dyke Association
West Street, Knighton,
Powys, LD7 1EN
01547 528753

The ODA produces a yearly *Where to Stay* booklet (a 'must have' for valuable information)
They also sell detailed route notes South to North and North to South; a castles alternative from Monmouth to Hay; strip maps of the path at 1:25 000 scale and a mileage chart

Baggage Carrying Service
01497 821266
If you want to do Offa's Dyke in style, staying in good hotels and having your baggage carried, try Acorn Activities, 01432 830083, or check their website at www.acornactivities.co.uk

DISTANCE CHART (cumulative)

	MLS	KM	COMMENTS		MLS	KM	COMMENTS
Chepstow				A489 Bluebell	95	153	pub closed at present, B&B
(Sedbury Cliffs)	0	0					
Bigsweir	10	16		A490 for Forden	101	163	pub only
Redbrook	14	23	pub only	Buttington	107	172	pub only
Monmouth	17	27		Llanymynech	117	188	
Llantilio Crossenny	26	42	pub only	Trefonen	120	193	inns
Pandy	34	55		Froncysyllte	133	214	pub, shop/PO
Hay-on-Wye	51	82		Llandegla	144	232	
Gladestry	62	100	pub only	Clwyd Gate	150	241	motel, B&B only
Kington	66	106		Bodfari	161	259	
Knighton	80	129		Rhuallt	166	267	inn
Churchtown	91	146		Prestatyn	174	280	

Irish Sea to Bristol Channel

Snowdonia to Gower

Over the Mountaintops of Wales

You've done Wainwright, you've done the Pennine Way, and you're fit as a fiddle, so what next? Well, why not dig out that tent and try Snowdonia to Gower? The mountain route's tougher than all the other routes outside Scotland, but, if it all gets too much, there are low-level alternatives, and you could always try B&B-ing it. To most walkers Wales means Snowdonia, and as such little of their attention has been focused on outlying areas to the south. Yet Wales has so much more to offer. An expedition that links the famous high mountains with lesser-known and surprisingly varied countryside must surely be a rewarding one, and Snowdonia to Gower does just that. It starts on the pebbled beach of Llanfairfechan on the north coast. Here the great grassy whalebacks of the Carneddau descend to the town's back yards.

below: On the Carneddau high route at Pen yr Helgi-du, looking down to the low route at the pass, Blwch Trimarchog. Both routes have an easy stroll from here into the valley at Ogwen

The route has three distinct sections. First is the high mountain traverse of Snowdonia to Machynlleth; then there's the rolling green hills and little-known valleys of Central Wales, which give way to the pastures of Llandovery. By the time you're ready to tackle the third, the great sandstone escarpment of Mynydd Du (the Black Mountain), you should be able to stride over it with the ease of a seasoned backpacker. Mynydd Du looks a bit like the Brecon Beacons, but it isn't encumbered with the Beacons' crowds, nor does it have any of those badly eroded paths. It's a great way to say goodbye to the mountains of Wales before descending to the coastal plains. So after 200 miles (320km) of craggy mountain ridges, windswept moors and idyllic wooded valleys you'll reach journey's end on the cliffs of the Gower Coast.

right: Climbing through the rugged cwm of the Afon Llynedno above Nantgwynant

Snowdonia to Gower started as a two-week holiday for me and my nephew Roy. The first crossing started in Aber, which lies a little to the east of the official start-point at Llanfairfechan, and it started a little late, after a day at work and a long ride on the little green Crosville bus.

SNOWDONIA: THE MOUNTAINS WAIT

The black ball rolled slowly over the baize and into the pocket. Roy beamed. No rapturous applause followed: the pool room of the Aber Hotel was empty, and silent, except for the ticking of an old wooden clock on the wall. Through the window the skies had darkened.

This was to be the start of a 200-mile coast-to-coast walk across the great mountain ranges of Wales. Delaying it no further, we left the warmth of the hotel for the cool of the evening.

above: The cantilever on Glyder Fach. Often a dozen walkers will be waiting their turn to 'walk the plank' and pose for the obligatory picture

As we headed south along the lane, the streetlights flickered into life. A squeaky iron gate let us into the glen, then a narrow path led us into the darkness of a forest. After fumbling around for twenty minutes we escaped to reach the sanctuary of scree-covered hillside. At the head of the glen, the cascades of Aber Falls splashed down shadowy cliffs.

Across the screes, a tricky bit of rock reminded us that we should have been here at least an hour earlier, but soon we were strolling through the remote corrie of the Afon Goch above the falls.

At ten our eyes were making harder work of the darkness than our feet were of the terrain – no moon here to light the hillsides, just fading torches. Stomping our boots into the invisible nothingness that was the ground, we found by trial and error a firm pitch for the tent.

Morning sunlight transformed the mysterious marshlands back into the high moorland corrie we had been expecting. But what a long corrie this was, and what a climb to the ridge! Somehow my rucksack seemed to weigh more than it did yesterday.

We made the ridge at eleven and were soon striding the grassy Carneddau whalebacks onto the stony 3000ft plateau of Carnedd Llewelyn. From here you can look back to the Irish Sea, and look forward to Snowdon, whose pointed summits peer over the Glyder range.

By mid-afternoon we were down in the valley again, at Helyg. Tryfan soars into the clouds – a giant wedge of rock and scree just waiting to be climbed. Beneath it, the dwarfed orange tents of a campsite promised the comforts of a loo, running hot water and the possibility of a bar meal at nearby Capel Curig. But these were to be Spartan days. I had been searching the map for an idyllic wild campsite high in the mountains and had come up with Braich y Ddeugwm, a rugged spur next to Tryfan.

Climbing the spur's tangled moor grasses and gritty slabs of rock, I was again hampered by the weight of my rucksack, and I lagged some distance behind Roy. A luxurious grassy shelf to lie on, views across to Tryfan, and sizzling sausages made up for the hardship. Braich y Ddeugwm was indeed good.

Looking for a toothbrush, I found four cans of lager at the bottom of my rucksack. Roy looked sheepish. 'Fosters: I thought you'd like them.' He had stowed them there the previous night. 'They weren't heavy, were they?

Tomorrow starts with a morning on the Glyderau. A scramble over boulders led to Glyder Fach. We were the first there, and had the whole fairground of rock to ourselves. First, the Cantilever, a gigantic slab supported at one end by vertical pillars. Next in line was a huge pile of boulders forming the summit cairn, and finally, Castell y Gwynt (Castle of the Winds), a wall of spiky rocks, and the start of the rollercoaster. You swoop down over boulderfields to the col, climb back up to Glyder Fawr, then plunge to the depths of the Pass of Llanberis. Just when you think it's all over, you look up and see the ramparts of Snowdon.

Doing Snowdon and the Glyderau in one day proved to be a bit of a grind, and I felt like checking my rucksack for bottles or cans. Snowdon's little steam trains, and the afternoon trippers in sandals, were wounding our pride by racing past on their eager ways to the summit. The hurt turned to frustration as the café closed its doors, leaving us to descend into the depths of Nantgwynant without the cool beer we'd been expecting.

The next stage was easy by comparison. We followed the old Welsh Highland Railway track through the gorge of Aberglaslyn, tackled Cnicht (a rugged little hill known as the Matterhorn of Wales) and descended to the green fields of Ffestiniog, where we saw another of those fascinating little narrow-gauge steam trains.

On the Rhinogau there's more fun to be had. Purple heather masks a heart of stone, and a mischievous heart at that. Loose boulders lie in wait for their chance to roll you over onto your haunches, and great transverse canyons, only hinted at on the map, make progress tiresome and route-finding troublesome. And yet you always forgive the Rhinogau their mischief: they're so different to the rest of Wales, and they let you get to grips with bare rock without the fear of falling from great heights.

We had a great time scrambling up and down the rocks, but by the time we were onto the easy grass of Diffwys and Llawlech we were more than ready to stop and admire the Mawddach river as it meandered among sandbars to the sea. It seemed to be as lethargic as we were.

Roy, never the one to capitulate first, looked relieved when I suggested a B&B at Barmouth.

'I suppose we could make an exception: after all, we've done pretty well today.'

The weather broke: maybe the gods were angry that we had succumbed to worldly comforts. We had crossed the Mawddach estuary on the mile long (1.6km) foot-and-railway bridge and were about to set foot on Cadair Idris when the skies burst open. Idris himself was

below: Castell y Gwynt (Castle of the Winds) is just one of the many rock features of the Glyderau peaks

warning us to keep off his seat. Boulders slithered beneath our boots, and grassy tracks were converted into rivers of mud.

As we took the summit, the clouds parted. Far below Idris's cliffs, a couple of steel-grey tarns drifted in and out of vision through swirling mist. We marched down to the soft green fields of Dysynni valley, past an old Welsh castle, and into the little village of Abergynolwyn. Now only the Tarren hills barred the way to Machynlleth.

Forest plantations have all but engulfed the Tarrens, and the Sitka spruce we walked among were hung with damp mist. Eventually the tree cover parted to reveal the slate rooftops of Machynlleth. We two ragged warriors hobbled and squelched through the streets in search of another B&B – a place to dry out, rest and recuperate.

above: On the upper slopes of Cadair Idris with the rock crest of Cyfrwy in the background

left: Glowylyn and Rhinog Fawr. The Rhinogs provide the most fun of the walk. Here, in a land once frequented by highwaymen, you can get to grips with bare rock without the fear of falling from a great height

ACROSS THE ELENYDD

We were halfway across Wales. The rocks of the North had disappeared behind the conifers of the Dyfi Forest. They were to be replaced by softer rolling hills of the south.

The rain pounded Machynlleth's shiny main street, where market traders sheltered beneath their tarpaulins. For them, and for us, it was to be a long, hard day.

Paths threading through dripping conifers led to a wide cart track over soggy ridges. Somewhere in the middle of a thick mist was Pumlumon, where the great Severn and Wye rivers begin their journey to the Bristol Channel. Nineteenth-century traveller, George Borrow, drank from the rivers' sources, but today, finding drier places seemed more important – just finding Pumlumon and the way off it afterwards would be good enough.

Compass work got us over the tops, out of the high winds, and through the ever-pounding rain to make it down to the Wye Valley. After an extravagant three-course dinner at the Glansevern Arms we needed to appease the mountain gods, and perhaps earn some good weather – so we camped on high amid some of the most malicious tussocky ground imaginable.

Maybe it worked, for the next day was easy and rewarding. The overnight rains had filled the streams of the Elan Valley so that their waters were roaring down the stone-built reservoir dams. Sunlight gradually showed itself between the boughs of lakeside oaks as the clouds dissipated behind the high moorland skyline.

Now when clouds dissipate, Roy has a habit of tucking spare clothing loosely under the

above: The confluence of the Doethie and Tywi rivers. This area between Llyn Brianne and Llandovery is perhaps the least known and most beautiful part of Wales. Here, you can see red kites and buzzards scouring the surrounding oak-clad rocky peaks for their prey

left: Carreg-ddu, one of the Elan reservoirs. The green track threading between the shoreline and the bracken is the former line of the steam railway that was built to carry materials for the construction of the dams. Today it's a fine path used by this Snowdonia to Gower route

right: Pennard Cliffs, on the Gower Coast, with only a few miles to go, and by now you're motoring on pure breeze-blown salt air. It's one of the best finishes to any coast-to-coast walk – but I'm biased, I suppose

straps at the top of his rucksack. On this day the item was a waterproof jacket. But a branch from some impish tree robbed Roy of his jacket.

The inevitable rain arrived at Elan Village. A rucksack liner came to the rescue, doubling as waterproof after holes were cut for head and arms. Wearers do get wet arms and get to look like bedraggled spaniels, but that's better than a wet everything.

Llyn Brianne lies to the south of the Elan reservoirs. Surrounded by plantations of spruce and larch in two narrow valleys, it mimics a Norwegian fjord. The splendid countryside beyond could only belong to Wales. Here the boisterous Tywi and Doethie rivers twist and turn among rocky, oak-clad peaks. Beneath a particularly conical hill called Dinas, the rivers meet in a violent cauldron of foam. There's a cave in the crags, where Twm Sion Catti, the Welsh Robin Hood, used to hide from his enemies. We didn't find it. But I did see my first red kite soaring above the woods and the summit rocks. These lovely birds were, in the last century, common on the streets of London, but had been hunted to near extinction, before their recent reintroduction.

After being in the Elenydd wilderness for three days, finding the Royal Oak at Rhandirmwyn was like finding an oasis in the desert. After a lunchtime tipple of Welsh Bitter and plates of piping hot *chilli con carne* we ambled down country lanes to Llanddeusant, where a low-level campsite provided an excellent overnight rest before tackling the Black Mountain.

It was good to be among real mountains again, but these mountains were not black at all: they were red! Their rugged sandstone cliffs were layered with gritstone strata. The climb to the tops, which rise to over 2600ft (790m) at Fan Brycheiniog, was delightfully easy, as was the grassy spur of Fan Hir, which descended right to the door of the Tafarn y Garreg Inn. Unfortunately, it was mid-afternoon and the door was closed.

Now battle-hardened, we decided to keep going across the little urban hills on the north-west side of the Swansea Valley and get as near to the coast as we could. In semi-darkness we pitched the tent by the shores of the Upper Lliw Reservoir. Through the steam of crunchy pot noodles, we watched the wind whip up white horses across the lake. The day's efforts meant that we could go for the coast a day ahead of schedule, but it would need an early start.

TO THE COAST

The quiet world of the golden Lliw Hills allows the first real glimpses of Gower and thus strengthens the resolve to press on – an ambition aided by superb paths over smooth terrain. These moors were the last high ground of the route. The remainder would be across the flatlands of Gower, through woods, across fields and to the coast. Small landscapes, but pleasing landscapes, too.

The going was fast: at four we were on the Gower Coast at Pwll du. Pwll du means Blackpool, but there were no crowds, donkeys or candy floss; just a limestone headland, a storm beach of white pebbles, and a couple of cottages.

Spurred on by the bracing coastal air and sight of crashing waves against the rocks, we completed the clifftop finale to Three Cliffs Bay. Climbers with their eyes to the skyline grappled with shoreline crags, and a links golfer was lining up a putt with his stern eyes to the ground.

Watching the surf bubble beneath my wrinkly, blistered feet I couldn't help wondering why I put myself through this when the climber was having such fun on his piece of rock. I watched the golfer miss his put, then throw his putter to the ground, and I had my answer. I would do it all again next year.

Snowdonia to Gower: The Route

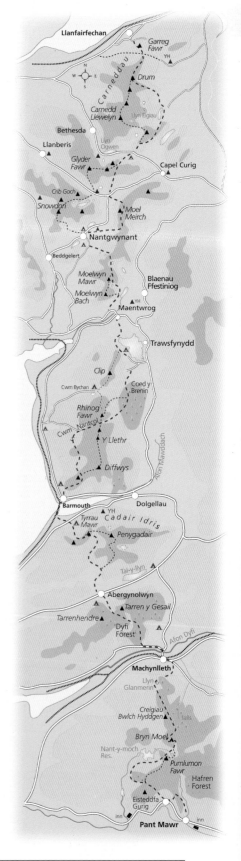

LLANFAIRFECHAN TO THE OGWEN VALLEY

Start the day on the pebble beach. Maybe it's good to let the surf flow through your toes, but behind those Victorian seafront hotels, the Carneddau hills wait!

■ Through the streets of the town to the outskirts at Pentre-uchaf, a winding country lane leads to the foot of the hills, and a stony mountain track (GR682739). Within 1½ hours you've reached the old Roman road, and within 3 you're standing on your first mountain, Drum, looking back to sea.

■ If the weather closes in, avoid the ridge between here and Carnedd Llewelyn. A low-level route turns E of Drum onto Pen yr Castell, then down into the Dulyn and Eigiau valleys, before climbing out to Bwlch Trimarchog and thence down to the A5 E of Llyn Ogwen. If not camping at Gwern y Gof Uchaf (opposite the path), go to Capel Curig, 3 miles W along a nice track running parallel to the A5. There are inns, cafés and a youth hostel.

■ If the weather is clement there's no reason to go low, for the Carneddau throw out superb grassy ridges. This is skyline travelling at its best; highest peak of the day is Carnedd Llewelyn (over 3400ft). Now the best route heads across to Pen yr Helgi Du, then down the grassy spur of Y Braich straight into the jaws of Ogwen.

THE OGWEN VALLEY TO NANTGWYNANT

■ Behind the campsite at Gwern y Gof Isaf, climb the spur of Braich y Ddeugwm from a signpost marked Llynnau Caseg-fraith. There's no real path but it's good fun, on tufty grass and flinty rock slabs. Small lakes at the top mark a diversion between the high and the low routes – the **low route** traverses the grassy pass, then clambers down rocky slopes to the Pen y Gwryd Hotel. It then climbs pathless slopes to Carnedd Y Gribiau before heading S along a heather and rock ridge to Llyn Edno. Follow the Afon Llynedno down to Nantgwynant (youth hostel, B&B and campsites), or find one

of the many romantic corners between here and Llynnau'r Cwn (the dog lakes).

■ The **mountain route** climbs to rocky Glyder Fach, then to the slightly less rocky Glyder Fawr. Take the sharp descent to Pen y Pass before tackling Wales' highest mountain, Snowdon, via the Pyg Track. Snowdon's S ridge provides the best means of descent. At Bwlch Cwm Llan the route turns E, descending to join the Watkin Path to Nantgwynant.

NANTGWYNANT TO TRAWSFYNYDD

■ Regain the Moelwyn-Siabod ridge by way of the path past the cliff-hung Llyn Llagi to Llyn yr Adar, a large tarn with an island in the middle.

■ From a cairned col beyond the far shores of Llyn yr Adar, a faint path descends to the vast old slate mines of Bwlch Cwmorthin, where the mountain and main routes diverge.

■ The **low route** follows the slate path to the left of the big slag heaps up to a high col between Moelwyn Mawr and Moelwyn Bach, then drops to the Stwlan Reservoir. A sketchy path leads down to the larger Tanygrisiau Reservoir by the banks of Nant Ddu. Follow the southbound bridleway by the Ffestiniog Railway and through lovely oakwoods to Tan-y-bwlch. Lanes lead to Maentwrog village then up towards Trawsfynydd Reservoir. At Bryntirion (GR680391) a track heads S into some conifers, followed by a path heading for the Trawsfynydd dam. After rounding the lake the route finds a path above the western shores leading to a tarmac lane which, in turn, leads to the long footbridge across the lake into Trawsfynydd village (campsite, B&B and inn).

■ From Bwlch Cwmorthin the **mountain route** heads SW on a sketchy path to Llyn Croesor, then climbs along the rocky spur rising to Moelwyn Mawr's summit. Continue along the connecting ridge, Craig Ysgafn, then to Moelwyn Bach via a little scree path on the left. Retrace steps to the bottom of the scree path then follow the lower route down to Tanygrisiau Reservoir.

TRAWSFYNYDD TO BARMOUTH

■ Recross the footbridge across Trawsfynydd Reservoir to follow the little tarmac lane towards Cefn Clawdd, but leave it for a track descending to the Afon Crawcwellt at Wern Fach. Climb the rugged slopes to a gate in Coed y Brenin Forest (GR675315). Turn right where a winding path meets a flinted forestry track.

■ At the concrete bridge over the Afon Gau (GR673287), the **low route** turns right on a path out of the forest, then through Bwlch Drws Arduddwy, a narrow pass between the peaks of Rhinog Fawr and Rhinog Fach. It comes to the green pastures of Nantcol. Follow the marked bridleway over the shoulder of Moelfre and into the desolate Ysgethin valley to the little packhorse bridge, Pont Scethin. Beyond the bridge the old London-to-Harlech coach road, a green track, climbs to the southern Rhinog ridge. Scale Llawlech, then leave the ridge for the track down to Sylfaen farm, where a little tarmac lane winds down to Barmouth (campsite, hotels).

■ The **mountain route** leaves the forest earlier, following the signposted path towards the Roman Steps. At the foot of the Rhinog rocks (GR600299), a narrow path on the left climbs through the heather to Llyn Du. A boulder chute is the start of a steep path to Rhinog Fawr. From the summit descend SE, rounding the little marshy hollow that overlooks Bwlch Drws Arduddwy. Turn back S to climb past Llyn Cwmhosan to reach Llyn Hywel. Here you tackle Y Llethr, highest of the Rhinog range. Follow the smooth grassy ridges to the cliffs of Diffwys before turning W over Llawlech to join the low route.

BARMOUTH TO MACHYNLLETH

■ Barmouth Bridge takes the route across the spectacular Mawddach Estuary and to the foothills of Cadair Idris. A narrow lane climbs to the twin lakes of Cregennen, where you have a steep climb to the shoulder of Tyrrau Mawr. Here, the main and mountain routes diverge.

■ The **low route** descends on a gravel

track into the valley of the Dysynni at Gwastadfryn. Take the lane past the castle of Craig y Bere to Pont Ystummer, which lies beneath the strange rocky peak, Craig yr Aderyn. A bridleway twists through the now tight Dysynni valley into the old mining village of Abergynolwyn (accommodation).

■ The **mountain route** over Cadair Idris climbs Tyrrau Mawr, then continues along the ridge over the rocky shoulder of Cyfrwy to the main summit Pen y Gadair. Retrace your steps to a junction of paths. Take the one S and climb Craig Cau. Follow the ridge fence to Mynydd Pencoed, then descend steeply to the footpath S of Pencoed Farm. Descend to the track parallel to the banks of the Afon Cadair, meeting the main route at the cottage of Tyn-y-ddol.

■ Follow a very steep lane from Abergynolwyn's village square up into Nant Gwernol, where it becomes a stony track ending at the quarries of Bryn Eglwys. The signposted path continues through the Dyfi Forest to Pont Llaeron, a medieval packhorse bridge said to have Roman origins.

■ The path turns left, parallel to the stream, to reach a high col (GR719056) between Tarren y Gesail and Foel y Geifr. Dyfi Valley Way signs guide you down an afforested spur on grassy rides, then S past the ruins of Pantyspydded on a less-defined forestry track.

■ At the 5–way junction of tracks (GR729033) take the one just left of straight ahead, SW to the edge of the forest near Bron-y-aur. A tarmac lane leads down to Dyfi Bridge and the road to Machynlleth (inns, B&Bs).

MACHYNLLETH TO PANT MAWR

■ Pass the ornate Victorian clocktower and Owain Glyndwr's old parliament building to follow the Llanidloes Mountain Road for a short way, then climb by the edge of a golf course to the forest that caps Parc (the hill). Continue over a stile through the top corner of the forest before passing Glanmerin Lake. On descending past Glanmerin Farm head S on a track to Bwlch Farm. This track continues along the ridge and through more forest at Rhiw Goch, then out above the cliffs of Creigiau Bwlch Hyddgen.

■ On rounding Bryn Moel the now indistinct bridleway

descends to the sheep sheds at Hyddgen, then continues S through the wild Hyddgen valley, almost to the headwaters of Nant-y-moch Reservoir. The climb to Pumlumon Fawr (Plynlimon) begins on a path by the banks of the infant Rheidol. By the southern shores of Llyn Llygad-rheidol climb through grassy gaps in the corrie's crags to reach a saddle between Pumlumon Fawr and Pumlumon Fach. It's a simple walk on a grassy slope to the top.

■ The best way down is via the S ridge to the forest plantation at Dyll Faen. If you've booked accommodation in Dyffryn Castell or Ponterwyd, continue down the ridge to the A44, otherwise descend E via the gravel track to Eisteddfa Gurig.

■ Avoid the busy A44 and reach Pant Mawr (inn, the Glansevern Arms) by climbing the Lechwedd Hirgoed ridge into the reedy Cyff valley. After fording the Cyff another gravel track takes you by the River Wye to Pont Rhydgaled ½ mile short of Pant Mawr.

PANT MAWR TO ELAN VILLAGE

■ At GR853821 descend from the A44 to cross the footbridge over the Wye, pass Nant Farm and climb forest tracks to the Bryn Du ridge. Stay inside the forest boundaries as barbed wire blocks the bridleway at both entry and exit points of the open fell. Descend past the hut at Nant Rhys to the banks of Afon Diliw. By the ruins of Lluest-dolgwiail, climb the hillside to Craig y Lluest for a wonderful view down the craggy Ystwyth Valley. Follow the Elan Valley scenic road to the bridge at Pont ar Elan, then cut across open moorland to a fading track along the E side of Craig Goch Reservoir. When it disappears pick up a stony track (the marked RUPP), which passes the huge stone dam before continuing by Penygarreg Reservoir.

■ After passing the second dam the

track comes down to the road again, but another track descends through conifers to the old railway track, providing a fine route by Carreg-ddu's shores. This leads to the causeway and road at the head of the most southerly of Elan's reservoirs, the Caban-coch. The Elan Village Hotel lies about 1½ miles to the E along the road.

ELAN VILLAGE TO RHANDIRMWYN

■ From the hotel, descend to the old village, take the suspension bridge across the river, then turn left on a good track to the Caban-coch dam. A path across boulders traces the shoreline before climbing parallel to Nant y Glo and the forests of Gro Hill. After swinging right, high on the hillside, a path traces the top edge of the forest, before descending to the farm of Llannerch Cawr. From here it enters the Rhiwnant valley by a bulldozed track.

■ Now the low and high-level routes diverge. The **lower route** stays with the track, climbing S to the windswept moorland pass of Bwlch y Ddeufaen. A fainter path descends to the shelter and stone cairns of Carnau and into the forestry plantations of Cefn Garw. A bridleway continues out of the forest over high fields to a farm track running SW past Glangwesyn and along the hillslopes of Bryn Clun to the Abergwesyn road. Turn right along the road through Abergwesyn, where the two routes meet again.

■ The **high route** stays with the Rhiwnant valley, fording the stream

---

Key to Maps

- – – – Main route
- ········· alternative route
- ▲ youth hostel
- ⋀ campsite
- ▲ mountain/hill top
- † church or abbey
- ♜ Castle
- 🌲 forest or wood

and following it past old mines. It climbs close to the Rhiwnant's source, before traversing tussocky moors S to Drygarn Fawr's summit, topped by two gigantic beehive cairns.

▧ Descend more tussocky ground into the rocky Gwesyn Gorge. A track soon develops, taking the route S to the Abergwesyn road, ½ mile East of the village.

▧ Across the bridge over the Afon Irfon, climb a flinted forestry track to the edge of the huge Tywi Forest. Do not enter here, but head SW past a huge house (formerly a hotel), then alongside a moorland stream. This vague path climbs to a moorland col, then drops down to one of Llyn Brianne's long fingers of water.

▧ A road takes the route round the S shores of the reservoir. At the Dinas RSPB Reserve a nature trail leads around the wooded hill of Dinas, and by the boisterous waters of the Tywi. It emerges back on the road. Another farm track, across the road-bridge at GR773460, hugs the foot of Craig Alltyberau and leads to a little lane beneath the crags of Y Foel. Follow the lane to the Tywi Bridge Inn (GR767446). There's a small campsite here, a larger one down the lane at Rhandirmwyn, a B&B at Nant y Bai Mill or the Royal Oak Inn, Rhandirmwyn.

RHANDIRMWYN TO LLANDDEUSANT

▧ Climb a forestry path from the lane N of Tywi Bridge Inn, before descending into Cwm-y-Rhaiadr. After meeting the Cilycwm lane climb the little hill, Penfedw Fawr, for a lovely view into Mynydd Mallaen's rocky cwms, then descend into Cilycwm village.

▧ Lanes lead to the bridge, Pont Dolauhirion, with a riverside path into Llandovery. Routes to Llanddeusant trace little-used lanes to Myddfai, a beautiful village with a fine little church and an equally fine pub, the Plough'. Further up the lane is another pub with a campsite, then, at Llanddeusant, a youth hostel.

LLANDDEUSANT TO THE AMMAN VALLEY

▧ At Llanddeusant the old red sandstone cliffs of Mynydd Du (the Black Mountain) bar the way into South Wales.

▧ Most walkers will want to tackle the magnificent **mountain route** over Bryn Mawr to Bannau Brycheiniog, highest summit in SW Wales. Here, turn W and follow a magnificent clifftop course over Bannau Sir Gaer before traversing the limestone outliers from Foel Fraith to Tair Carn Isaf. From here drop into the Amman Valley, once famous for its anthracite coal mines. The direct route descends to Glanaman, but there is more choice of accommodation in Ammanford.

▧ The **low-level route** follows the bridleway past Carreg yr ogof and into the Twrch valley where there are two river crossings (easy in summer: wet feet at any other time). Paths over the Afon Twrch to Rhiwfawr continue over the squat, semi-urban hill, Mynydd Uchaf. A lane leads down to the A474. Accommodation is available a bus ride away at Pontardawe or in the Amman Valley (paths also traverse N up the valley to Glanaman). If you're on this low route it would be best to book B&B at Coynant (Ceunant GR649071). To get there, lanes climb the Lliw hillsides to Penlle'r Castell, where the Amman Valley routes of the next day are joined.

THE AMMAN VALLEY TO THREE CLIFFS BAY

▧ Today you need to climb to Mynydd y Gwair in the Lliw Hills, S of the Amman Valley. A little lane climbs from Glanaman to Banc Cwmhelen, where paths lead across the bare hills to the high lane and the earthworks of Penlle'r Castell. A long, winding lane from Ammanford arrives at the same place.

▧ Well-defined tracks continue across the moors of Mynydd y Gwair and Mynydd Garn-fach before reaching a high lane above Cwm Dulais. Another track descends into the valley, rejoining the lane just beyond some pylons. The lane descends to the B-road halfway between Pontardulais and Gorseinon. Half-a-mile S along the road, follow a lane to Grove End Farm, then go S along a path that keeps to the W of Gorseinon. On meeting the A-road continue S along streets to Gowerton before finding pretty paths through woodland and fields to the lane at GR582955. A couple of hundred yards S along the lane, the route traces a track SW into Dunvant.

▧ From Dunvant the redundant LMS Shrewsbury railway has been made into a walk/cycleway, and it goes through the trees for 3 miles, where it emerges at Black Pill on Swansea Bay.

▧ There are better places to finish Snowdonia to Gower further W; follow the promenade to bustling Oystermouth, where the route turns inland on a short stretch of road to Langland Bay. Here begins a breathtaking finale of coastal paths on sandy beaches and high limestone headlands to Three Cliffs Bay, where there's a castle, half buried in the sand dunes, and where you turn inland for accommodation or the bus home.

DISTANCE CHART (cumulative)

	MLS	KM	COMMENTS		MLS	KM	COMMENTS
Llanfairfechan	0	0		Abergwesyn	123	198	shop only
Roewen YH	6	10	YH only	Bwlch-y-ffinnr Llyn Brianne	129	208	B&B only
Helyg	14	23	campsite only	Rhandirmwyn	135	217	
Pen y Gwryd	18	29	inn only	Llandovery	144	232	
Nantgwynant	25	40	YH	Myddfai	147	237	inn only
Maentwrog	35	56		Llanddeusant YH	153	246	YH
Trawsfynydd	41	66		Cwm-twrch Uchaf	163	262	shops only
Barmouth	56	90		Ceunant (Coynant)	173	278	B&B only
Abergynolwyn	67	108		Pontardulais	177	285	
Machynlleth	73	117		Black Pill (Swansea Bay)	187	301	
Eisteddfa Gurig	89	143		Parkmill (Three Cliffs Bay)	197	317	
Elan Village	95	153		Rhossili	209	336	
Rhayader	114	183		(Gower Extension)			

ESSENTIAL INFORMATION
Start: Llanfairfechan
Finish: Three Cliffs Bay
Distance: 209–16 miles (336–45km) depending on choice of routes
Total Ascent: 45,000ft (13,725m)
Time: 12–16 days
Terrain: Serious mountain paths in Snowdonia and Mynydd Du (the Black Mountain); moorland paths and tracks in Central Wales; more complex route-finding on field, woodland and coastal paths in South Wales

above: A wintry Fan Brycheiniog with Llyn y Fan Fawr peeping out from behind

MAPS AND GUIDES

OS Landranger 1:50 000 Nos 115, 124, 135, 147, 160 and 159. These maps are good for general hillwalkers but are not as good as OS Outdoor Leisure and Explorer maps 1:25 000 which show field boundaries and greater detail. Unfortunately the number of maps and the price would be prohibitive. A good compromise would be to take OS Leisure Maps 16/17 (one map), 18 and 23, coupled with Landrangers 135, 147, 160 and 159

A Welsh Coast to Coast by John Gillham (Cicerone Press) – a practical pocket guide
Snowdonia to the Gower by John Gillham (Bâton Wicks) – a coffee table guide

TRANSPORT

Llanfairfechan has a railway station on the North Wales coastal line and is also reached by bus (Crosville Wales Ltd, Imperial Buildings, Glan y Mor Road, Llandudno Junction, Gwynedd LL31 9RH. Crosville run services across much of

Wales). If you want to do a half of the walk only, Machynlleth and Barmouth have a railway link to Shrewsbury, Aberystwyth and Porthmadog. Buses run from Parkmill near Three Cliffs Bay, and Rhossili to Swansea. Swansea has an Inter-City railway station and reasonable bus links to the rest of the United Kingdom

TOURIST INFORMATION

The main year-round tourist offices are:
Caernarfon 01286 672232

Porthmadog 01766 512981
Dolgellau 01341 422888
Machynlleth 01654 702401
Llandrindod Wells 01597 822600
Llandovery 01550 720693
Pont Abraham 01792 882828

Bristol Channel to English Channel

Uphill to Old Harry

From Weston-super-Mare to the cliffs of Dorset

I n England, in the zero years, you no longer need to be a master architect like Wainwright to build your own walk. You can do it with prefabricated parts taken off the shelf. When I wanted to walk across the SW peninsula I lifted down the *Long Distance Walkers' Handbook*, the OS map index and the OS maps. I found the West Mendip Way lying ready to my hand, needing only a few corners knocked off (and a few more knocked on). The Monarch's Way I could use, and the Macmillan Way, with a little bending, could be made to fit into place. Finally I could lay down as many miles of the Dorset Coast Path as the project needed. And there I had it: my DIY Way across the south-west.

It won't necessarily work in Wales, and the Scottish Highlands are a different game altogether. But anywhere in England you can do it. The south-west turned out to be a good choice, but in walkers' England, good choices aren't hard to make.

To walk from the sea on one side to the sea on the other side is such a fine idea that I never felt any temptation to follow Thomas Hardy or the Tolpuddle Martyrs, or trace the boundary of the chalk. A lesser theme was the set of limestone towns, mostly equipped with cathedrals – Wells, Glastonbury, Sherborne, Dorchester. However, the pier at Weston-super-Mare, splendid as it is, doesn't really fit that scheme.

I wasn't altogether happy with the geology: limestone is nice, but this is almost all limestone, and what isn't limestone will be chalk. However, limestone does come in various shapes. First, the small but lively Mendip Hills, next, the cow meadows and small green humps of Somerset; Dorset would be long ridgeways over the chalk, and finally the spectacular Dorset coastline.

below: The Mendips rise out of the sea at the Church of St Nicholas at Uphill, just south of Weston-super-Mare. The first of the walk's ready-made paths, the West Mendip Way, now leads over the hills to Wells

THE MENDIPS: HILLS WITH HOLES IN

On Weston pier you walk on boards with the sea lapping under the gaps. You walk with piped music and at the end you turn and choose between the boards round the other side and the dodgem cars and grab-a-teddy machines through the middle. Weston Beach is busy, though with long bleak views across the mud to Wales. It's a brash and strident start to the walk.

Things quietened down once I'd wandered up to Uphill and joined the West Mendip Way at the cliff-top church of St Nicholas.

The Mendip waymarks are tall oak posts, and plenty of them. Each waymark tells you how far it is to the next place, how short a distance you've travelled since the last – but in August, fortunately, the part of the post with the depressing measurements is lost in the long grass.

Under the low sun, Somerset is a bright pattern of fields and hedges, with a little hill called Brent Knoll sticking up out of it. Brent Knoll is familiar to travellers on the M5, just beside the Sedgemoor Services. It's even more familiar to south-west walkers: it's going to take three days to walk past this small hill.

Crook Peak is an upstanding summit with steep sides and a rocky top. So what if it's only 600ft (200m) high? The views are huge, and a low-altitude mountain ridge leads on over Wavering Down and into a wood whose small-leaved alders indicate it to be part of the ancestral Saxon scrub. The Way wanders round the edge of Shipham and then I leave it in order to grab the high point of Somerset.

On this walk 1065ft (325m) is as high as we're going to get. Beacon Batch is a moor of heather and gorse with little paths running around in all directions while wide green tracks pace in a more dignified manner towards the central trig point. A bridleway leads back to the West Mendip by way of Gorsey Bigbury. It's only when I drop into the wooded limestone valley that a notice-board suggests there would have been a better way by Long Wood, which is a nature

above: On Wavering Down, where the long green ridge of the Mendips leads in from the sea

reserve. Spend time before the walk phoning for leaflets and you discover these things. Never mind. The Black Rock nature reserve is also a good walk: it's a limestone valley with woody bits that burgeon and flourish like nobody's business. Once across the road, I leave the Mendip Way again in order to tremble along the brink of the Cheddar Gorge.

Here are walkers of the short-distance sort: in city clothes with their lunch in a carrier bag. 'Is it all downhill from here?' It is, but the drop through the wood of slippery stones will be more demanding than any climb. How convenient, though, to get a holiday's-worth of adventure from 2 miles of Cheddar cliff-top, and spend the next six days on the beach. But I'll be on the beach, too, soon enough – the viewpoint tower at the bottom helpfully indicates that Bournemouth, though out of sight, is a mere 55 miles (88km) distant.

Cheddar is a vulgar spectacle surrounded by car parks. There's an underground fairytale with fibreglass monsters that glow in the dark. There are stalagmites and stalactites all floodlit in orange and yellow, and a clever trick where they make a pool at eye level so you see it all twice over. Outside there are ice creams, and vertical limestone crags rising straight out of a layby. If we want understated classic landscape, we'll get that on the Dorset ridgeway, and at Sherborne Abbey. Cheddar is cheesy, and jolly good fun. Before lunch and on a weekday, it is only moderately overcrowded.

We continue along the southern flank of Mendip. Slanty grassy bridleways have views over the very wide, very flat Somerset Levels. Brent Knoll refuses to get any further away, but Glastonbury Tor is gradually getting closer. At Priddy they moved the market from Wells to avoid the Black Death and never got round to moving it back. Priddy has a stack of symbolic market hurdles made of chestnut wattle under a straw roof. Alongside, in August, they make the real market of rusty tubular steel and blue string.

Dropping towards the Ebbor Gorge I met an elderly walker navigating by the sun who requested a look at my map. He was walking the Mendips to scatter the ashes of his late wife in the places that I too was visiting: Uphill Church, Crook Peak. He told me not to worry about old age. 'They've just given me a titanium knee and it works just fine.' He also told me the best way in the Ebbor Gorge, which is not along the top edge.

SMALL HILLS OF SOMERSET

The wide, wide Somerset plain has fortunately at this point become rather narrower. Between the last of the Mendip outliers at Pennard Hill and the first of the green lumps at Castle Cary, there will be seven flat miles – and some of them are spent in woods, so you don't really feel the full flatness. Beyond the plain, the green lumps of southern Somerset are

left: The Mendips have gentle rounded tops, but the bottoms are spectacular. The route leaves the West Mendip Way to teeter along the brink of Cheddar Gorge

below: Ebbor Gorge. Here the path follows a former stream bed and gets the view that the water got as it went over the edge

small but cheerful. You walk a narrow strip of nature reserve or mud (depending on the season) and look through a grown-out hedge down a sudden grassy slope to chequered fields and another cheerful green lump, and a golden village with a pub in it selling cider.

Wells is the first of three limestone towns along the route. The Early English cathedral stands as a 200ft waymark where we join the Monarch's Way. The cathedral has a story-board west front: a display of disciples, prophets and all the nine Angelic Orders that constitute the 'Poor Man's Bible'. After 30 miles (50km) of foot travel it becomes easier to shift perspective through the centuries and realise that in its cheerful excess of decoration, this is the fourteenth-century equivalent of Cheddar Gorge or Weston-super-Mare.

Those who know their Gothic architecture will point to the silver-grey stone of the lower columns and say 'Purbeck Marble, typical of the Early English of course'. It is indeed; and over the last five miles of our way we'll be walking on that Purbeck stone.

I left Wells westwards through dreary suburbs, heading for Callow Hill and Glastonbury. The first field footpath was unpromising: a strip of thorn with nettles under. At best the Glastonbury dog-leg involves flat places and lanes. Add to this unusable footpaths and it no longer seemed

above: Looking forward into Dorset from Cadbury Castle. Various places, from Tintagel to Shropshire, and even Edinburgh, think they've been lived at by King Arthur. Cadbury is the most plausible Camelot claimant

left: Wells is the first of three limestone towns along the route

worth pursuing, even given its healing well, its Arthurian romance and its Tor. So I went back into Wells to take another photo of the cathedral and look for the reserve route: the Monarch's Way.

This straighter route leaves Wells wonderfully, along the moat of the Bishop's Palace (where the swans have learnt to ring a moat-side bell when they want their dinner) and straight out into the countryside. On a gatepost under an oakwood I found the first of the Monarch's waymarks. These are white roundels, no bigger than the King's own shilling, scattered here and there but by no means everywhere

What is it, this Monarch's Way? It's a route of 600 miles (950km) – which is about 500 miles (800km) too far. Its idea is to follow the escape route of Charles II after the battle of Worcester – which is only a slightly exciting idea. Its route is a series of messy dog-legs, triangles and double elbows that finally emerges at Brighton, having successfully evaded all its enemies but the stinging nettle. It's a route that I'm not at all tempted to pursue, and, judging by the secret state of the stiles, neither is anyone else.

Somerset is lush and squelchy. It is vigorously green. Every square inch of this ground has been, at some time in the last ten years, a fresh cow pat. Somerset has its own smell, and if you get too deeply involved in its softer, browner aspects you may never be able to face a frothing pint of full-cream milk again.

The path passes a cow, and a vineyard, and three pubs, and several more cows. It climbs Pennard Hill by a sunken lane, and at the top it shows you Brent Knoll, still not out of sight, standing against the sunset.

There's one place in the flatland I've been looking forward to. There's going to be a real river – the Alham, a tributary of the Brue – and an ancient bridge to cross it on. I push through thistles onto a bit of stony path, and I'm half way across it before I even notice the river Alham. The stony path has a sudden edge, and below, in a hole among the thistles, is some yellow-green water with weed on. Crowded alders mean it's impossible even to see the bridge from more than nine inches away.

So much for the river crossing. But the bridge leads to a path below a hedge, and eventually, after a passage between stalks of sweetcorn that meet overhead, the Monarch crawls – thistle-pricked but not demoralised – into Castle Cary.

Castle Cary is biscuity limestone with a fine market hall, and behind it is a hill. You look back with satisfaction across the Somerset plain, with the Mendips a grey distant shadow. Pretend not to notice the Bristol Channel in the distance: after this the Bristol Channel will be out of sight forever. And southward are the small green hills of Somerset.

Here various paths – the Monarch's, the Macmillan and one called Leland – twine together like mating snakes. Leland is a local authority short trail, following a grumpy monk who walked this way in Tudor times. The Macmillan Way celebrates, and raises money for, a very worthwhile cancer charity. Again, though, I wouldn't want to walk it, for the walk's idea, which is to follow the limestone for 212 miles (340km), seems to me a wrong one. That said, Macmillan is very useful to us here, and better waymarked than the Monarch was.

Cadbury Castle is a place to linger, to lie in soft grasses looking at one or two of its views, and wander around the rim, and lie in some more soft grasses and look at another of the views (but not perhaps the one that, very annoyingly, still has Brent Knoll in it).

After Cadbury I left the named Ways, and took footpaths onto Corton Hill and along the

left: Somerset, seen from Corton Ridge at dawn. Look at this picture very quickly and try to avoid noticing that Brent Knoll is still not out of sight

Poyntington Hill that is the Somerset and Dorset boundary. Crowded contours on the map suggested that this would be a route with a view: and the contours were not wrong. Up on that hill, though, Dorset played its trick on me. Somerset's trick was the nettle-bed stile: Dorset's trick is a sunken lane, green and easy, where you put away the map because there's nothing to see but hedges and realise, when you come to a crossroads after a mile of rapid downhill, that it's the wrong sunken lane.

Sherborne has a lake, and a castle beside the lake where Sir Walter Raleigh once lived, and an abbey that matches Wells Cathedral.

DORSET: LONG CHALK AND A RUDE MAN

Dorset is the chalk, and the chalk forms gentle ridges that you pass along very fast. A phrase from one of the historical novels by Rosemary Sutcliffe sticks in my memory (for no better reason than that there was a boy called Ridgeway in my class and so it was useful for teasing purposes): 'the long green Ridgeway that stretches from World's End to World's End'. But first, there's another low bit to get across.

Blackmoor Vale is only 7 miles (11km), and the first three are a straight bridleway heading south out of Sherborne. This is an ancient road, obviously: but like your early classmates, it's all gone different ways. For a while it's a farm track, or someone's drive; then it's grass and wild flowers between hedges, and a muddy streak in a wood; and then a bit that's kept right on being a road and is now tarmac and tractors. It gets me halfway across the flat bit.

And for the rest of the flat bit I've got my Explorer Map and I'm ready for some exploring. The Explorer Map (the new 1:25 000 that replaces the limp green Pathfinder) shows field boundaries, and claims to know which side of the hedge is the right-of-way. And so, feeling like Stanley and Livingstone in my Explorer shorts, I track – not the elusive lion but the elusive line, the green dots of the footpath. I hunt down the stile gap, work out what fences are too new to be on the Explorer, and trace – like the faint footsteps of the antelope – the vestigial marks of a hedge that once was, and which, according to Explorer, still is.

And then there's a wood with nettles and brambles, and me still in the explorer shorts. Do I stop and change into trousers, or do I hope the brambles are only as brief as my legwear? Nettle-stings are less effective in August when the plants are old and big. And some of the stings are 2ft above the top of my head: they aren't going to hurt me at that height ....

The nice thing about a flat bit is that you don't have to climb far to get a view – 200ft (60m) up Telegraph Hill, and there's half a county to look at, all green with hedges and pasture. Over the top the colour changes. It's the chalk, and chalk land is dry land, divided into brown squares of plough and dusty yellow squares of wheat. The ridgeway is fast and seductive, 9 miles (14km) continuously downhill from here to Dorchester. It's easy to imagine yourself, in skins and some sort of fur bikini, striding out for Verulanum or Duvernum to have a good laugh at those weird Romans, pilfer some bits of their foreign

right: Middle Bottom. The Dorset coast, with its relentless ups and downs and relentless heat, turns out to be ideal training for the glaciers of Aconcagua

jewellery, and stride home again. The combine harvester is at work below the Cerne Abbas Giant – the monster machine no larger than one of the Giant's chalk-carved testicles.

The first fellow-walkers since Cheddar were on the paths around the toes of the Giant, but soon I was alone again up on the ridgeway. The ridgeway path runs along a hedge with views down a green dell and across brown and yellow squares to the Hardy Monument above Weymouth. A mile later it switches to the other side of the hedge, and then, across a different green dell and the same brown-and-yellow, there's a horizon shadow that must be the hills of Purbeck.

At the back of Charminster come the walk's first few yards of river-bank, and at the back of Dorchester there's nearly a quarter-mile more. And that's the walk's riverside bits out of the way. Dorchester has what looks like a castle, but isn't – it's a Victorian military museum – and what looks like a heap of earth, but is in fact a castle. The Maumbury Rings are a green hollow, to rest in and remember Cadbury; but all around is the noise of the unseen town, and the railway line's just behind the rampart, and then some children arrive to claim the green hollow to play cricket in. So I stopped remembering, and went out through the housing estate to find the path across the bypass.

The path here is another ready-made walk, part of the Jubilee Way. The Jubilee isn't the Queen's, but that of the Ramblers' Association, so the path is bound to be a good one. This particular bit is a hard chalk track that slyly insinuates itself into a fold in the landscape and makes its way below cornfields and small woods. Bridleway signs suggest that, with the sea somewhere just behind Came Wood, the walk should here reach its conclusion. For having started at Uphill, where else to end but Came Down? However, where walks are concerned, language does not take priority over action. The Dorset coast ahead is more important than any place-name, no matter how persuasive. So, at the foot of Came Wood, I turned aside from Came Down and headed east for Culliford Tree.

THE DORSET COAST: CHALK ERECT

It's taken a long time to walk away from the Bristol Channel. Almost half way to Bournemouth, the sea could still be seen behind. The English Channel, though, arrives quite suddenly at the corner of Came Wood. It was after sunset when I came to Came, and the sea was darkness except for a red glow along the horizon and the street-lights of Weymouth reflected in Portland Harbour. Portland Bill itself is an urban island, its steep shape twinkling with the lights of radio masts, ancient limestone castles and the Young Offenders' Institution. I unrolled my bivvybag on the stubble of White Horse Hill so as to look at Portland Bill all night.

The Ridgeway, yesterday, was chalk lying down. The Dorset coast is chalk standing up on end, 300ft (100m) high. I lingered taking photos of the first spectacular cliffs at Ringstead Bay. No photos of Ringstead Bay illustrate this account. The cliffs at Middle Bottom and West Bottom and Swyre Head made the spectacular cliffs of Ringstead seem rather ordinary. And then came Durdle Door ....

Well, the Dorset coast is pretty well-known, and I was a lucky walker not to have done Durdle Door before, and to come to it under early sun that sparkled off the English Channel onto the underside of the arch. While Lulworth has outdoor cafés where the same lucky walker can sit under the same sun and see it sparkle on the surface of a chilled fizzy drink.

Through the Lulworth ranges the path goes up and down, up and down, from soaring clifftop

to pebbly beach, so that you do thousands of feet of ascent without ever more than 500ft of altitude. There are lots of walkers: casual walkers in rolled-up trousers, cool walkers in bikini tops. The walker I stopped to chat with was the one with the big rucksack. He turned out to be in training for Aconcagua. Up and down, up and down in August heat in Dorset has certain significant factors in common with the Patagonian glacier he told me, and had I noticed the butterflies?

The white cliffs were starting to vibrate in the midday heat. The sea was an extravagant blue, the limestone grass a strident green: a seaside scene as painted by a very young person using poster-colours in unspillable tubs and a big brush. It's hard work, this Patagonian glacier, so I stopped at the last beach for a midday swim. The beach was a pebbly one, a little sore on sensitive foot-bottoms, but the sea was a delight, and the white chalk made a three-quarter circle with a tall yacht in the opening.

Research doesn't always help. 'Go by the coast, it's wonderful,' said my father, who lives in the county, and who's been walking a lot longer than I have, obviously. 'Go by Corfe Castle, it's great,' said my friend John – and John is the ex-treasurer of the Outdoor Writers' Guild. Well, the coast would have to be very good indeed not to be an anticlimax after Durdle Door, and I was tempted by the prospect of a range of hills. So I left the vigorous up-and-down at sea-level for the flatness of the high ridge. The ridge was the Kimmeridge, which draws back half a mile from the English Channel in order to see even more of it. Hang-gliders glided and hung in the updraft of its sudden edge; mountain bikes trundled along its top.

above: Chalk ridges allowed Celtic Man to make long fast routes all over southern England – though the motorway service station came later. Chalk also let him form the earliest and rudest graffito of all. The Cerne Abbas Giant is known to his admirers as 'Big Willy' on account of being 180ft tall

overleaf: Durdle Door. Here the Purbeck limestone comes ashore. Its harder rocks form the ridgewalk that ends at Old Harry

The broken turrets of Corfe Castle erupt from the tightly-clustered chimneypots of the ice-cream shops. Corfe Castle the village has a steam railway and its own range of hills, the famous Purbeck limestone. What more could you ask?

Well, you could ask for the hills to be a little bigger. The Purbecks rise to 653ft (199m), barely above the topmost stone of the castle. A busy track runs along the top. There are walkers of all sorts up here, as well as horses. I fall in with a chambermaid from a local hotel, hitting the hills before the dinnertime rush. She's a runner, and a hillwalker, but has yet to try the combination sport. Do you need a special rucksack to go running in the hills? No, you only need one with a waist-strap.

Well, that's not quite all. You also need an obsessive attitude to training, and the ability to enjoy foul weather, twisted ankles and getting lost. 'And you've got everything for the night in that little rucksack? What do you do about clean clothes?'

'Stand downwind – then you won't need to ask.' After that, the question of why there are so few women in fell-running hardly needs to be asked.

The chambermaid goes off down the side to her dinner-guests. But I keep right on to the end, to where the hungry sea is licking away the tip of the Purbeck Hills as a hillwalker licks his choc-ice. The end of the Purbecks is Old Harry and his Wife – two great pillars of limestone stand out in the entrance of Poole Harbour. The pillars have holes in, and so do the high cliffs of the mainland, and evening walkers stand unsuspecting on smooth grass with the sea grinding away directly below their feet. There's a little path leading out to the final point of Purbeck and the end of my south-west walk. In the photos I'm posed on the first, rather than the final, hump. Well, I have occasionally come across mountain ridges that seemed to be vertical on one side and overhanging on the other. Here, though, the paradox actually happens: there is indeed a hole through underneath.

Falling off the edge would, of course, be the ultimate in dramatic endings to a walk. It would also avoid the question of what next: the sand to Poole or back down the coast to Swanage? The Sandbanks Ferry runs late into the evening, so I kept going eastwards. The sun sank into the purple heather of the Nature Reserve, and over my shoulder Old Harry and his Wife gradually turned grey, then black, and lights came on on the Isle of Wight. And a notice rose out of the sand of Studland Beach. I was to Beware of Naturists.

No naturists at this time of night, fortunately. Unless I myself …? It was great to get out of the sweaty clothes, and the night air was most refreshing. It wasn't so nice getting back into the sweaties, as beach litter and sandcastles indicated the approach of the other end, and the streetlights shone on the water. The chain ferry came rumbling out of the darkness to take me over to Poole.

above: Corfe Castle invites comparison with Castle Cary, back in Somerset. Both are beige sandstone, flower-baskets and confusing bendy lanes. Corfe wins out by actually having a castle

right: The Purbeck Hills finally fall into the sea at the crumbly rocks of Old Harry and Old Harry's Wife. The weary walker, with 100 miles of Somerset and Dorset behind, should be careful not to do the same ….

Uphill to Old Harry: The Route

WESTON TO WELLS
■ From the pier at Weston-super-Mare, head down the beach for 2 miles (3km), turn inland to Uphill and climb to its church. Head south for 400yd/m to join the West Mendip Way. This is well way-marked and will be followed to Wells with just four diversions. The first, just after the crossing of the M5, is a brief detour to visit Crook Peak.

■ After Shipham we branch off to the high point of Somerset. From a small reservoir at GR457573, follow waymarked forest tracks through Rowberrow Wood onto Black Down, then take paths past the summit of Beacon Batch and SE to a gateway (GR490569). After another 100yd/m, turn right onto a field path down to Lower Farm; a track on the left, just before the farm, is a nature trail (permitted path) through Long Wood.

■ Cross the B3135 at the head of Cheddar Gorge, and follow the clifftop, to S of the gorge, to the edge of Cheddar village. Turn left on a lane to rejoin the WM Way at Bradley Cross.

■ The West Mendip Way leads on through Priddy to a wood above Ebbor Gorge. At a cross-path above the gorge, where a West Mendip Way sign and one 'to Car Park' point ahead, turn right to descend the better route inside the gorge. Rejoin the WM Way to Wells.

WELLS TO SHERBORNE
■ Leave Wells on the little-used and lightly waymarked Monarch's Way, starting at the Bishop's Palace. Use the Explorer map and a compass to work out where the path goes.

■ At Castle Cary move onto the well-marked Macmillan Way. Just before North Cadbury (GR637280) turn right across a stream, keep ahead into a green track and at once turn left on a field path. Take the Monarch's Way round the W edge of the village, thus avoiding a nasty crossing of the A303.

■ From Cadbury Castle the Mac Way leads to Sherborne; a more interesting route takes field paths by the Beacon on Corton Hill, Poyntington Hill (GR656202) and Oborne to enter Sherborne past the Old Castle.

SHERBORNE TO DORCHESTER
■ The little-used paths across the Blackmoor Vale require care; some of the map's field boundaries have been removed or altered. Leave the town by a path opposite the station, passing to E of Longburton (GR657126) to a chapel just S of the village (GR651121). The field path now running SW is tricky, and at GR647113 has been diverted slightly S of the map's line.

■ Bridleways run SW onto White House Common, then turn left (SE) for 1 mile (1.5km), and S along a wood edge to a phone box and Pond Farm. Take the footpath (not the bridleway) up Telegraph Hill. Turn left beside the road for 400yd/m to a bridleway running down the ridge of East Hill to Up Cerne and the Giant Viewpoint on the A352 near Cerne Abbas.

■ A path leads up W through Cerne Park to the track that runs S along the chalk ridge, leading straight to a junction just S of Crete Hill. The route forks left to follow bridleways over Charminster Down to Charminster. A field path leads to Burton, and after a brief but busy road a riverside path

on the left runs into the back of Dorchester.

DORCHESTER TO POOLE
■ From Dorchester's Maumbury Rings, streets run W to a housing estate (GR700897). A path at the bottom of Balmoral Crescent crosses the ring road to Came Park. The Jubilee Trail runs S to a corner of Came Wood (GR696858). Turn left to reach a road junction. A wide track runs SE to the trig on White Horse Hill.

■ The ridge-crest bridleway, signed 'Inland Coastal Path', passes Pixon Barn to Moigns Down. Descend E into a dry valley to reach Holworth. A bridleway runs S to join the Dorset Coast Path at Holworth House.

■ Follow the spectacular Coast Path past Durdle Door and Lulworth and through the Lulworth Ranges. One mile (1.5km) after Worbarrow Bay the path branches (GR889797). Keep straight ahead and follow the high ridge 1 mile (1.5km) inland, passing above Kimmeridge to Swyre Head; turn sharp left to a car park and the road into Kingston. A field path runs N across Corfe Common to Corfe Castle.

■ Go down to right of the castle and under the railway. A path climbs

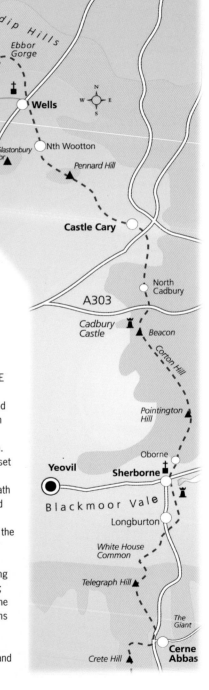

steeply onto East Hill, then runs along its crest to join the bridleway on Rollington Hill. This runs over Nine Barrow Down and Ballard Down, to reach the walk's end-point at Old Harry Rocks.

ESSENTIAL INFORMATION

Start: Weston-super-Mare, Somerset
Finish: Poole, Dorset
Distance: 120 miles (190km)
Distance on roads: 18 miles (29km)
Total ascent: 14,000ft (4200m)
Time: 8 days (of 15mls/ 24km), but there is accommodation to suit any speed
Terrain: Countryside and small hills. The route is mostly on paths and tracks, but with some tricky routefinding across fields

ACCESS

Paths through Lulworth Ranges are usually open only at weekends and on Bank Holidays. Check with Tourist Information or phone 01929 462721

DISTANCE CHART (cumulative)

	MLS	KM	COMMENTS		MLS	KM	COMMENTS
Weston-super-Mare	0	0		Sherborne	58	93	
Uphill	2	4		Longburton	61	98	inn only
Bleadon	5	8		Cerne Abbas	70	112	
Shipham	14	22		Dorchester	79	127	
Cheddar	20	32	YH	Osmington (+2ml)	86	137	
Draycott	23	36		Lulworth Cove	94	150	YH
Priddy	26	42	inn only	Kingston	104	166	
Wells	31	49		Corfe Castle	105	169	
North Wootton	34	54	inn only	Swanage (+2ml)	111	177	
Steanbow	35	56	inn only	Old Harry Rocks	112	179	no facilities
Hornblotton	40	64	inn only	Studland	113	181	
Castle Cary	44	71		Sandbanks Ferry	117	186	
North Cadbury	48	77		Poole	120	192	
South Cadbury	50	80	inn only				

MAPS AND GUIDES

Explorer (1:25 000) 153, 154, 142, 129 and Outdoor Leisure (1:25 000) 15. The lines of the West Mendip Way, Monarch's Way etc are marked on these. *West Mendip Way* by Andrew Eddy, pb Weston-super-Mare Civic Soc (from Wells TI)

TRANSPORT

The start and finish are served by stations at Weston-super-Mare and Poole. There are intermediate stations at Castle Cary, Sherborne and Dorchester (all with trains to London). Local buses link many points of the walk with Bristol, Sherborne and Dorchester. A small steam railway links Corfe Castle with Swanage (timetable **www.swanrail.demon.co.uk** or phone 01929 425800). At the walk's end, the chain ferry runs across the mouth of Poole Harbour constantly between 7am and 10pm

TOURIST INFORMATION

Weston-super-Mare
01934 888800
Wells 01749 672552
Sherborne 01935 815341
Dorchester 01305 267992
Weymouth 01305 785747

Swanage 01929 422885
Poole 01202 253253

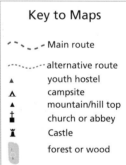

Key to Maps

- – – – – Main route
- ·········· alternative route
- ▲ youth hostel
- ⋀ campsite
- ▲ mountain/hill top
- ⛪ church or abbey
- ♖ Castle
- forest or wood

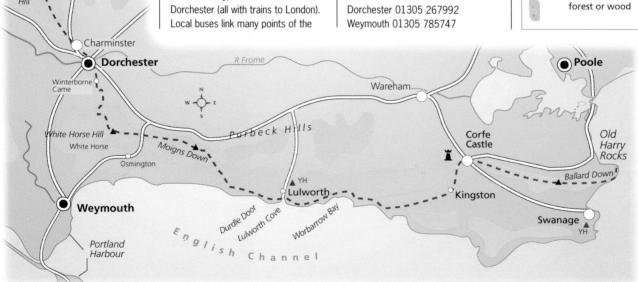

Atlantic to North Sea
Highland and Grampian

THE TWELVE PASSES

This is a route through all the mountains of Scotland: but it is not a mountain route. It's a through route that's also a route through, and it devotes itself to the old-fashioned idea of the high pass. To walk between clouded mountains along a golden river that gradually, gradually, diminishes to a stream; to climb a stalkers' path into a rocky col; to drop into a pinewood as the weather breaks; and then to collapse dripping and weary in the bar of some ancient inn – and then to do the same thing again tomorrow, and the day after – this makes for a very satisfying way across a country.

There are, it turns out, at least twelve different ways of finding a gap between some hills and walking through it. Glen Nevis is a valley-wander between mighty ranges, while the crossing to Glen Tromie takes you over a bleak moor where there's nothing to see but sky. Cloich-Airde is a gloomy inescapable defile: the Lochnagar crossing is a complex weaving among the very summits.

Low may be the way to go: but in Scotland, low can end up higher than you think. The route crosses two Corbetts, and goes within a whisker of a minor Munro that should never have been let into the tables. But it's a logical (or in the case of the Lochnagar crossing, almost logical) line of least resistance, and its nights are spent in bothies, bunkhouses and even the occasional civilised village.

MALLAIG

Mallaig is a practical sort of place. If they want a 50ft fridge on the end of the pier then they build one, and never mind if it blocks the Cuillin. The Cuillin are in cloud, so who cares? Meanwhile the land view is tarmac and concrete, scattered here and there with bits of dead fish.

OK, so the sun's not shining. And I did arrive by a train trip that was

right: The mountains of the West rise steeply out of the sea by rock and bog and lochan. Here, on the slopes of Knoydart's Beinn Bhuidhe, we look out over Loch Nevis towards Skye. For the short first day to Sourlies, this hill provides a fine-weather alternative to the path over the pass of Mam Meadail

above: The rough mountains of Knoydart, seen from the south. The route follows the mist-filled hollow of Cloich-airde. Splendid Sgurr na Ciche rises behind

right: The first day's walk is over, but we're still at the seaside. Looking back along Loch Nevis, with Sourlies bothy just ten minutes away across the pebbles

definitely spooky: grey rain and darkness descending, and the dark shadows of mountains, with inky black bits that were lochs, or the sea. The last passenger got out at Arisaig and it was just the driver in a cubby at the front (and what was a continuous view of black loch and grey mountain, delivered at a steady 30mph, doing to *him*?), the guard in a cubby at the back, and me. The line ran up against a low concrete building and stopped. The train hissed and was still. Outside was wind, and seagulls, and a few streetlights reflecting in salt water. The sun wasn't shining in Mallaig. But then, it usually isn't.

The Knoydart peninsula, just north of Mallaig, is one of the few places in Britain you can't get to in your car. You arrive, from Mallaig, on a Monday, a Wednesday or a Friday, on Bruce Watt's boat the *Western Isles.* You leave the same way, or else you walk, and the walk is a long one. It's 20 miles to anywhere else at all, and those miles are some of the most mountainous in Scotland. When the men came home after the Kaiser's war they repudiated the landlord and declared a Workers' Soviet on Knoydart. And just two weeks before I got there it happened again, only this time funded by the National Lottery. Knoydart has altered for ever; for on the deck of Bruce Watt's boat is a man in a suit, trying not to notice the mountains and talking into his mobile phone about the stock market.

    The mountains are hard to ignore, rising into the cloud in a series of confident rocky bounds that indicate they're going a whole lot higher before they stop. The clouds are blowing around and regrouping: they are about to abandon their steady westward push and make a surprise attack from some completely new direction.

PASS 1: MAM MEADAIL (545M)

A pass is the least difficult way through; but least difficult doesn't have to mean easy. Mam Meadail is a pass of the classic sort. From the rhododendrons of Loch Nevis, a narrowing valley leads in among the hills. Water falls in on either side, and the valley gradually narrows and climbs to a skyline notch between two stormy summits.

I crossed the slabby ground at the head of the pass and peered down. Below me, a rainbow dived into a hollow and disappeared among the clouds. And then the clouds drew apart to show a sudden new valley, a silver river and a zigzag path to take me quickly down to that river's sheltered banks.

Sourlies Bothy is the first of the H&G Walk's 'Very Romantic Nightspots'. It's reached along the shingle, or at high tide by an awkward hip-hop above a crag. It stands at the head of Loch Hourn, surrounded by sea water, waterfalls and rocks. But it was only teatime, so I pressed on through the Mam na Cloich Airde.

PASS 2: MAM NA CLOICH AIRDE (315M)

This gloomy defile is where Hamish Brown came closest to abandoning his All-the-Munros Walk. Water splashes down the mountainsides, and straight out of the sky, into a long narrow loch that has a view, due to the bending in the defile, of nowhere. One leafless tree struggles out of the boulderfield. A dingy sunset creeps in from the western end. To the suggestion that the countryside should be a green and pleasant place, the Mam na Cloich Airde offers a hollow laugh. Black and ochre are the colours here.

Not all of the greyness was the intrinsic gloom of the pass. Without my noticing, night had started to fall. The valley out of the pass is more open, and there's a lot less gloom to linger and appreciate. I hurried down it, and at 8 o'clock saw the roof of the bothy 2 miles away.

There is, or there ought to be, a rule of late nights that says: if there's enough light to see the bothy from where you're standing, then there's enough light to get to the bothy from where you're standing. I just managed the final ladder-stile without needing to hunt out the torch.

A'Chuil is less romantic than Sourlies as it's in a plantation.

PASS 3: KINBREACK (455M)

No notch this, but a high wide place of streams and bog. In mist it's particularly bewildering. Do I steer by the streams? Streams run in all directions, including into my boots – and also down inside the legs of a useful pair of waterproof overtrousers.

Well, the trousers are purple ones, which is last year's colour. Also, the current beating them against the boulders has seriously increased the breathableness of the left leg. If you want to pick up the top-of-the-range gear you need to be on lower, more popular hills than these. The really good outdoor equipment is all being worn on the pavements of Ambleside.

Good, rapid tracks run along the soggy glen of Kingie to Tomdoun.

Is the bunkhouse at Tomdoun another of the Romantic Nightspots, or is it merely exceedingly inexpensive? It has the essentials – antlers, and green curly rustic woodwork; a windy porch for drying out your trousers; and a Highland inn just 10 yards away. It was built as a dosshouse for the builders of the Quoich Dam back in the 1950s, and whether for reasons of economy or nostalgia has not been upgraded since.

Everyone in the bar is either a fisherman or a hillwalker. The two sports stare at each

below: Stormy sunrise over Loch Garry at the start of Day Three. Those who walk up from carparks only see half of the hills. They miss the dawn and the sunset, as well as most of the really interesting weather

other across the fire, or engage in a little nervous fraternisation.

Yet another bunkhouse bonus is not having to wait around for any hotel breakfast. Instead of egg-yolk running across a greasy plate, a yellow 6am sunrise ran down the misted hills and pooled across Loch Garry. Yellow sky in the morning, shepherd feeling slightly unwell? Certainly it signalled dirty weather ahead.

PASS 4: GLEANN CIA-AIG (385M)

Cia-aig is a harsh pass. It was once a through-route for herds of black cattle that plodded and splatted from the darkening glens of autumn towards the slaughterhouses of the south. It's a brown and trampled place, and even today retains a whiff of the cowpat.

And yet it has its moment. That moment is the ruined croft-house of Fedden.

The path up curves in, and the path down curves away, and so Fedden is completely enclosed. Where the lower parts of the sky would normally be are curves of the big hill, and waterfalls, and stones. Here the cattle stopped for the night on a small green field surrounded by bog. And here starts a dry and fairly visible path, that gives quick glimpses of Ben Nevis and the Grey Corries before plunging into a scented pinewood.

The Caledonian Canal's towpath is a little too long, a little too wide and firmly surfaced. Feet just reaching their sixtieth mile of being wet may find it a trial. However, there is bright water on one side, yellow gorse and fresh birch-leaves on the other, and several more glimpses of Ben Nevis.

I'd booked into the Backpackers' Lodge in Fort William. 'Backpacker' here does not indicate someone with a large rucksack walking across the hills, but someone with an even larger rucksack doing Europe on 12 Euros a day. The place is a youth hostel, but with added frivolity. The notices telling you not to do things are done in vulgar-coloured inks. There's alcohol in the common room. I'm the oldest person there, and the only native Scot – indeed, the only Briton.

They assigned me a bunk called 'Mr Silly'. Remarkable insight into character, these non-British young people. Now if they'd given me 'Mr Jelly' I'd have been a bit insulted.

PASS 5: GLEN NEVIS HEAD (375M)

It was a perfectly routine rescue. Walking down Glen Nevis in the dark on the last day of March, we saw two lights above the Steall Falls. 'Can't get down there,' said Inken; and sure enough, the lights started to flash an SOS.

And so, for the first and only time, my hill-running skills were put to use in the service of humanity. Down Nevis Gorge I went at a fair old speed, stone to stone on the wide but rocky path. Water below showed white occasionally, and roared; steep trees flickered in the torch beam; and the echo in the air suggested precipices. I trotted down to the camp site and called the Rescue. Eighteen people had been up there behind the torches; one had fallen over a small cliff and hurt himself, though not badly. The helicopter fetched them out in the early hours.

above: The walk makes a southward loop along the Caledonian Canal – not just for the convenient shops of Fort William, but also for Glen Nevis. At the top of an almost-Himalayan gorge is the tremendous Steall Waterfall

above: The entertaining footbridge in Glen Nevis

Two torches among eighteen? Dear me. And obviously they hadn't studied the escape routes in advance. Very stupid, shouldn't be allowed onto the hill, should be made to pay for the helicopter. Lucky for them there were a couple of real hillwalkers passing by.

Well, let's take a look at those two real hillwalkers. Ice-axes, crampons, torches – but what's that on their feet? Running shoes? And what are they doing in Glen Nevis in the dark anyway? Thirteen Munros? Hmmm ....

Now let's flash back ninety years and suppose I'd seen those lights above Steall in 1906. Candles, they'd have been, in some wonky lantern that kept going out and when you tried to relight it, burnt your fingers. Back in 1906, I wouldn't have finished my rather challenging day by running for the Rescue. In 1906 I'd have turned myself round, gone back up Garbhanach for about 1000ft, across the steep rocky stuff, down the stream for about 500ft, and spent the rest of the night leading the eighteen back up the stream, across the rocky stuff, and down Garbhanach. That would have given me a really interesting night out, given the eighteen an appropriate dose of suffering in consequence of their bad mapreading, and cost the taxpayer nothing ....

Glen Nevis in the dark, and two years later, Glen Nevis by daylight – it's like the book, and then the film of the book. Usually, the film disappoints – they've cut the story, and the pictures aren't so good. But in Glen Nevis, the eye improves on the imagination. I'd never have visualised those huge boulders in the bed of the gorge. The slopes above the waterfall are smooth dirty slabs dabbed with loose vegetation. I'm a simple soul, and could never have thought of anywhere quite so nasty to get stuck in the dark with only two torches.

On our left now, the Grey Corries: on our right, the Mamores. This long valley runs in, past mountain after mountain, while the river alongside gets gradually smaller and the path alongside gets gradually lost in the bog.

After 10 miles (16km) a new river starts in the opposite direction, and a new path is gradually found, and you pass several more mountains. Along the way are two bothies, and at the end will be Corrour, a place reached by railway but by no road, with a bunkhouse and a youth hostel.

A stony but enjoyable track runs round the head of Loch Treig. Not enjoyable is the path that leads off it for the last 2 miles to Corrour. This becomes boggy, and then boggier. Finally it becomes underwater, with a few floating duckboards and much peaty slurry. If a frog can do it so can a person, surely? Black and dripping to the knee, I finally emerged at the Corrour bunkhouse.

For days, as I'd approached this place, people had been saying 'You're going where? Ah – Morgan's Den,' and sucking through their teeth. Sadly for the lovers of the sinister and the not altogether salubrious, Morgan is no more. The place has reopened under new management, and is now a simple Victorian signal-box, standing on the platform between the two lines of the railway, with clean comfortable bunk beds, and lots of heating. Oh, and the signalman's former control room where you can sit above the trains with a 360-degree view of misty hills.

In other words, this is the next of the journey's exotic nightspots. Though it's a shame that such a large part of the view should be occupied by Beinn na Lap, often considered as the least exciting Munro. (The outdoor writer Ralph Storer suggests that, to avoid becoming a Munro-bagger, you choose one you're deliberately not ever going to do. Beinn na Lap is an ideal candidate.) A smaller but better hill, Leum Uilleim, stands proudly behind the northward rails. Its bottom is in bog, its middle's in cloud and the very tip catches the last of the sun; it's a confection in pink and brown like one of those scented chocolates for Valentine's Day. 'The most romantic of the Corbetts,' says Morgan's successor. 'It's official, I read it in one of the books.'

PASS 6: THE BEALACH DUBH (725M)

It doesn't take long, surely, to cross a simple pass between two hills? Well, the Bealach Dubh, to the north of Ben Alder, climbs to almost 2500ft (750m) and shouldn't take more than a day. This is a pass of black peat and late Spring blizzards. Five miles of climb (8km) lead to a narrow place between two mountains, with a patch of old frozen snow. The cloud brushes the pass top, and grey scree and white waterfall tumble out of the cloud into the rather large river below.

The Fara is a long narrow hill that has nice grass to walk on and points in exactly the right direction. Alternatively, there's a harsh bulldozer track alongside Loch Ericht.

The two routes rejoin beside a fine eighteenth-century castle in Scottish Baronial style – at least, it will be a fine eighteenth-century castle just as soon as they've finished building it. After a mile, you pass the gatehouse: even more splendidly baronial, with an arch through the middle big enough for a troop of horses, a stretch limousine and indeed a low-flying Lear Jet. If pointy windows and pepperpot towers were good enough for Queen Victoria, then they're quite

overleaf: Heading east along the wide waters of Feshie

below: The hills of the East may be smooth and boggy-topped, but the East's valleys are steep and sudden. Glen Gaick is crossed on the sixth day

appropriate for a millionaire eccentric enough to spend his pocket money on Munros rather than a football team, say.

Dalwhinnie is not a pretty place. Heather hills rise slowly out of the bog and up into the cloud. The gentle slopes leave lots of space between for rain and wind. Spray thrown up by the lorries flies for hundreds of yards before splashing down in a peat-pool. The turrets of the distillery introduce a note of jollity, but, among the concrete of dams and aqueducts and the grim brickwork of the derelict hotel, nobody laughs. The one good bit is the interior of the Ben Alder Café.

PASS 7: BOGHA-CLOICHE CROSSING (800M)

below: Evening in Glen Feshie, and the welcome sight of smoke from the bothy chimney. The deer come down at dawn to graze under the Caledonian pines

We are now in the Grampian part of the journey. Instead of sharp summits and narrow ridges we have wide flat tops covered in heather and gravel. The high pass, instead of being a notch just under the cloud line, is a blasted peat-bog. Up on the hags of Bogha-cloiche there's nothing to see but flat dead grass, a few Cairngorms peeping over the rim, and the dial of the compass.

The summits of the east may be dull. The valleys of the east, though different, are different in an interesting way. Meall Odhar (Dun Hump) and its heathery hags end in a sudden plunge. Quite suddenly you're looking down slopes of scree and outcrop, cut by streams into lovely curves that lead steeply down into Glen Tromie.

A cunning stalkers' path sneaks in beneath the cornice remnant, trickles down a hidden fold in the slope, and hits bottom in convenient zigzags. Rivers like the Tromie move around like snakes at a disco – from the moor above you can see, like a geography lesson, previous riverbeds all over the glen – and this one has moved out from under the footbridge. I forded it, with ice-axe acting as a third leg. After heavy rain, though, a surprise extra trip upriver is required to see if the next bridge, 3 miles away, has also been destroyed or not.

PASS 8: TROMIE TO FESHIE (700M)

The heather in the high ground west of Feshie could be horrible. However, there are grassy little stream valleys, and just enough tracks and paths to get through. The layout is complex, at the watershed of Spey and Tay, and if the little stream valleys are not terribly dramatic, at least you keep dodging round a hill and peeping into a new, not terribly dramatic little stream. And the tracks and paths are fast, so that you arrive at the Feshie bothy half way through the afternoon and wondering what to do.

A particular pleasure is to arrive at a bothy and find some nice people who've lit the fire. They were Frank and Sandra from Bridge of Don, and they'd even brought a bowsaw for the logpile. They generously offered real food – a freshly-boiled potato – where everything I have has been hauled from Fort William. Bothy chat is of bothies, and wildlife, and which hill did you last get lost on? Soothing subjects.

Sandra and Frank are true bothy people. The main part of their bothy day will be spent gathering firewood for the bothy night. When he does climb hills, Frank does so as Munro himself: in his kilt. Quite comfortable, he says, cool and yet warm. But when it gets wet it chafes; and it's the worst thing in the world for falling suddenly into a stream.

Tourist Information leaflets give each hotel a line of little symbols to designate the facilities. That wouldn't work with bothies, as so many of the facilities are one-off. Ruigh-aiteachain has pine-log seats carved by the commandos during World War II. It has an underground earth closet involving some drainpipe and a chair with a hole in. It has the memory of a fresco painted by Landseer – this on a wall alongside that has now collapsed.

By dawn the fire's gone out – you'll just have to warm yourself in front of the sunrise. And in fact a Feshie sunrise can give you quite a glow. The map's green patches with fir tree marks are not forestry plantations, but remnants of Caledonian pine, with squirrels and martens running around in the branches. During the night the deer come down: the first person out in the morning should carry a camera.

PASS 9: FESHIE TO GELDIE (570M)

This pass may not be high; it may not be hard (Landrover tracks, mostly); but it is very, very long. The day starts well, with 4 miles (6km) of Caledonian remnant. The track is grassy; the woods are birch, juniper and ancient pine, with crags and waterfalls overhead and the roar of the great river in your ears.

A wide gentle valley leads gradually up into the empty country under the Cairngorms. The Royal Engineers have built a fine footbridge, crossing the Eidart River above a waterfall. It carries a cast-iron sign. Do not stoop to read this, as it tells you exactly how many miles remain to Braemar!

From the footbridge it goes steadily downhill – and this is metaphorical as well as literal. Another wide gentle valley leads slowly out again. The high summits of the Cairngorms lie so far back as to appear almost flat. After quite a lot of miles the path gives way to a Landrover track that really does go on for rather too long. The main interest is in wondering whether Braemar will arrive before nightfall, or vice versa.

At White Bridge the track begins to feel like the M25, as traffic out of Glen Tilt merges from the right, and then the busy trunk route through the Lairig Ghru arrives from the left, along with the River Dee.

A small road takes you alongside the Dee, surfaced with pine needles that are some relief to well-trodden feet. And the long day ends in beauty as it began, when a stiff climb leads into the Morrone Birkwood.

Up here, little peaty paths run through the heather and between the scattered birches and juniper. Behind the birches are the cragged corries of Macdui and Beinn a' Bhuird, the little knobs of Ben Avon. Above all stands the tall pyramid of Cairn Toul. Meanwhile, new leaves are golden-green at sunset and there's a large herd of deer standing around. It would be a bad mistake to come into Braemar along the road.

PASS 10: LOCHNAGAR (970M)

One or two of the Eastern Grampians are not completely boring. For instance, Lochnagar. A logical and sensible pass, mostly on good paths, leads from Braemar to Loch Muick through the Lochnagar massif.

Well, to be completely frank, it's not so much through as over. This natural pass line rises to 970m (3200ft) and runs just below a couple of minor Munros. It then dives into a descending bog-trough – what's going on here? Why aren't we taking the nice clear path over Lochnagar?

In the context of this walk, Lochnagar occupies the undignified position of Reserve Route for when the mist makes the bog-trough too tricky. The valley steepens; peat gives way to rock. There's a big crag on the left, a much bigger crag on the right, and the Dubh Loch below. The stream becomes a continuous waterslide over granite slabs. With a further waterfall streaking down Eagles Rock opposite, and the black loch below, it's a thrilling descent.

PASS 11: MARK MOOR (725M)

It's a gentle stroll around the south side of Loch Muick. Except that I looked at my watch, and my map, and had 7 miles and 2000ft to go (11km/600m), and three hours of daylight to do them in, and the lonely bothy to find at the end of it. This is another high moorland crossing, with the additional feature that you spend the night up there. Shielin of Mark bothy lurks at a nowhere-in-particular point somewhere among the streams and peat.

Three hours is plenty, so long as I don't make any silly mistakes. But it's nice to pretend that it isn't, and stimulate the walk by doing the odd bit of it at a spanking pace. It really isn't necessary to confirm progress with constant reference to the stopwatch. You only do that if you're playing the game of navigating as fast as you can without actually wasting any time in intelligent thought.

The final moor playfully interposes peat hags across the line of the compass-bearing. How close can you get to the bullseye? I was out by 200yd.

No track, not even a path runs to Shielin of Mark. The bothy book has sad tales of those who started too late and had to camp among the hags. A month before me, a party had failed to find the river despite much digging in the drifts, and had to melt snow over a stove.

Eskdale under the Scafells: Eskdale in the North Yorks Moors: Eskdale in the Southern Uplands – all are walking country that is pleasant or better. (In the case of the Lakeland one, much better.) Any of the Eskdales from source to civilisation makes a good long day. And the same goes for Glen Esk in the Highlands.

The Angus glens are grassy green, but rise in crags to bleak heather. Long stony tracks above and grassy paths below: this is the pattern of Clova and Isla and Prosen as well as of Glen Esk.

Glen Lee starts as a slight groove in the heather. But soon there's a babbling brook below and bits of crag overhead. The track twists around Hunt Hill to a sudden view of two precipices and the Falls of Unich. The valley twists again and widens, and the track leads out past Loch Lee to Invermark Castle. The first house claims to be a branch library. I didn't try to borrow a book, as a rather large fine would build up before my next visit.

A little-used road runs down Glen Esk – we're not going to walk on that if we can help it. Parallel paths run through the hill country to the north – I used them last time in Glen Esk, but this walk's had quite a lot of hill country already. So this time, I use the paths to south of the river. They run through small woods, and along the riversides, and past abandoned farms.

I crossed a final dangling footbridge and rose up the glen side to St Andrews Tower – a silly structure erected in 1826 for no obvious reason. Maybe it's just that the rounded hills hereabouts require a spike on top to liven up your Glenesk photos, as the sprinkle of salt on the porridge. The triangular one on the Hill of Rowan serves this purpose admirably.

PASS 12: MOUNT BATTOCK (778M)

Eastward it gets easier, and the best way to heighten the atmosphere is to heighten the height. So this final pass is actually a summit. (There's a genuine pass of 455m just to the south, on tracks over the Hill of Turret.)

On the long track up Mount Battock, the surroundings gradually go brown again as Glen Esk slips back into its fold in the hills. Lochnagar rises from behind the moor, and down in the south-east there's a faded blue line along the horizon. The sea is in sight.

Over the top of Battock appears a whole new landscape, as evening falls across the green fields of Aberdeenshire. Aberdeenshire hills are small but shapely: smallest and shapeliest, at the end of the next Landrover track, is Clachnaben of Glen Dye.

The track runs towards Clachnaben through country that is most interesting. The peat lies on a basement of decomposed granite gravel. The ground is pale grey, and firm enough that the Landrover track can go wherever it wants among the humps of black chocolate-coloured peat with heather topping.

The bothy's now just down on the right. Should you do Clachnaben today, or tomorrow? If your reply is 'not at all' then I must request you, now, to bury our book in the peat and make your own way out on the roads through nasty Brechin. This really isn't your sort of book. The reason to do Clachnaben now is to save 1000ft (300m) of climb back onto the ridge. The reason to do Clachnaben tomorrow is that without this interesting hill, tomorrow is going to be a long haul out to Dunnottar. Fading daylight may answer the question for you. If light is fading – stay high!

left: Loch Muick, between Lochnagar and the moors of Mark. Queen Victoria, who saw more of Scotland than most, preferred the gentle east to the more exciting mountains of Ross-shire. Her own 'wee bothy' of Glass Allt-shiel stands at the loch's head, below the waterfall path from the Dubh Loch

above: Granite, but not the Cairngorms. The small hills of Aberdeenshire provide light relief at the very end of the mountain ground. Bennachie, Buck of Cabrach – or, on this particular crossing, Clachnaben

Clachnaben at sunset is wonderful, and the descent track is clear by moon or torch.

I got to wonderful Clachnaben a full five minutes before sunset. But alas: somewhere in my haste I'd dropped the camera's main lens. I enjoyed the Clachnaben sunset as best I could through a telephoto lens. Clachnaben has rocks on top, with real rockclimbs on one side, a little scramble on the other and a cool eastern breeze blowing over all.

A lens in a little vinyl bag looks very like a lump of peat. Three times I see it lying on the path, and the third time, lucky me, the peat turns out to be vinyl after all.

Inside the bothy, a cosmopolitan touch is a wall-map of Arctic Canada. I sat on the patio under a silvery moon squeezing out my socks, and realised that my nearest neighbours were the ones passing overhead at 600mph in the sanitised discomfort of an airliner.

FETTERESSO FOREST

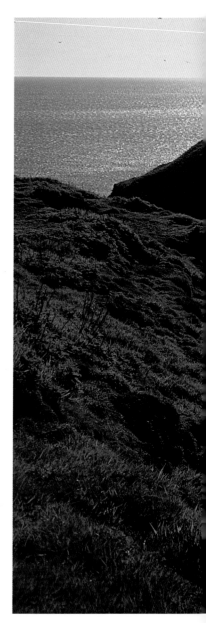

right: Ruined, massacred even, and collapsing into the sea: the walker at the end of twelve days of Highland and Grampian, and Dunnottar Castle

The bad part of any Highland crossing is the lowland section in the east. Scotland has rights-of-way, but not nearly enough of them, so roadwalking and beer-drinking – possibly over as many miles as 30 – are what must link the hills with the sea.

By heading for Stonehaven through Fetteresso Forest we reduce the roads to only 4 or 5 miles (7km). At the same time, sadly, we reduce the beer to zero. Intoxication – of the alcoholic sort – can only start at Stonehaven itself.

A small hill called Kerloch has a certain atmosphere with its tumble of stones, its view of sea and Lochnagar, and much foreground heather. Two hang-gliders were preparing to launch themselves off Kerloch – they let me hold some of the bits down while they toggled together other bits and tightened it all together. The obvious question: has anyone glider-hung coast to coast? It could be done, given just the right sort of wind and a lot of luck with rising air. Three or four people have managed to ride right across the Cairngorms, starting from the Glenshee chairlift.

All through the stuffy Fetteresso forest I nursed my memories of Clachnaben. Tracks not on the map provided mental stimulation; but I realised that the newer and smarter the track, the less likely it is to be marked, and then it was all straightforward. After three hours or so, I emerged blinking into the sunlight. Half a day on umber heather and pale grey grit: then half a day under blue-grey trees: the green of lowland pastures excites as a strange new colour. On Cheyne Hill I turned the final fold; and saw, on map and in real life simultaneously, the sea ahead.

Those who've negotiated Fetteresso Forest will not be thrown by the unmapped extra roads and houses in Kirktown. They will, though, be thrown by the noise, the industrial estates and the garden centres. I had trouble working out which way cars were coming at me from.

The central square of Stonehaven is a veritable crowded forest of exciting shops (food! socks! sticking plaster! fizzy drinks!) The old harbour is mostly made of stone and feels less alien. An alleyway climbs between two stone buildings onto the rocky clifftop.

The cliffs are a reddish conglomerate, crammed with rounded pebbles, like currants in a bun. The clifftop grass is yellowed over with primroses. Dunnottar Castle, comprised of tottering stonework, suspended paths and tunnels, stands on a peninsula that's almost an island. There are stone walls with holes to shoot people through, a spectacular gents' toilet poised over the abyss, and there was once a massacre here.

Where better to end ten days of all of Scotland?

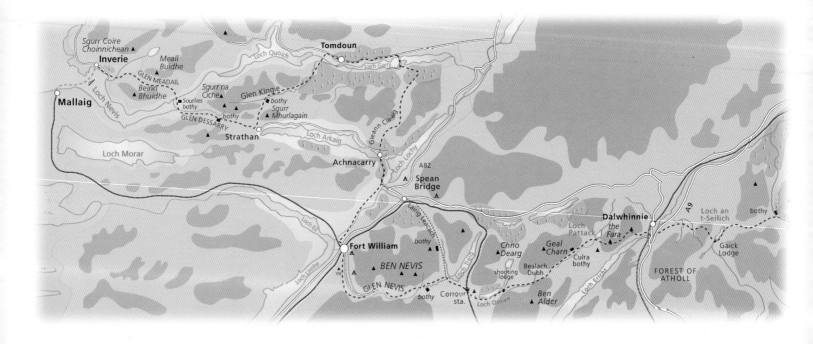

Highland and Grampian: The Route

KNOYDART TO A'CHUIL

■ From the edge of Inverie, a good stalkers' path runs E and crosses Mam Meadail to Carnoch. A footbridge (marked 'dangerous condition, use at own risk') is at GR866966.

■ Follow foreshore around the head of Loch Nevis to Sourlies bothy. A path leads E through Mam na Cloich Airde. At a forest's NE corner, turn down right to a footbridge and A'Chuil.

A'CHUIL TO TOMDOUN

■ Take a wet path to Upper Glendessarry, then track SE to Strathan. Cross the Dearg Allt, to find a small path NE marked by a cairn.

■ In the wide flat col the path is lost. Descend past Kinbreack to a ford of the River Kingie (GR001964).
Head up directly to the track above. This heads E into forest, to emerge onto the Glengarry road 1½ miles (2km) W of Tomdoun. Apart from the hotel, there's an interesting possibility of a ferryboat across Loch Garry to bunkhouse at Garrygualach.

TOMDOUN TO FORT WILLIAM

■ After 2 miles (4km) of road, cross Loch Garry on a long bridge and take tracks past Greenfield. At the crossing of the Allt Ladaidh (GR230003) turn right (S).

■ The track turns uphill beside Allt Bealach Easain and ends at a stone enclosure and a fence gate. Just above the gate a forest ride heads SW, with a faint path. Head down W to the ruin at Fedden.

■ The path down Gleann Cia-aig becomes a forest road. A forest trail down right (temporarily closed) short-cuts to the Eas Chia-aig waterfalls.

■ Pass through Achnacarry to cross the canal at Gairlochy to the towpath on the E bank. (Here the short-cut route continues ahead.) Follow the canal S to its end at Caol.

■ Turn onto the B8006, and cross the River Lochy on a long footbridge beside the railway. A riverside path leads to Inverlochy, a suburb of Fort William.

FORT WILLIAM TO CORROUR

■ Take the Glen Nevis road to fork off on forest road on its right after 3/4 mile (1km). It rejoins the road near Achriabhach. Later you can take a riverside path on either bank.
A built path passes through the Nevis gorge. Rough paths lead up the River Nevis to Meanach bothy at Luibeilt, then down the Abhainn Rath. Left bank is easier, unless you're heading for Staoineag bothy.

■ A track runs round Loch Treig and an extremely swampy path leads to Corrour station.

SHORT-CUT ROUTE: GAIRLOCHY TO CORROUR

■ This misses the Caledonian Canal, which is no great loss; the sparkling Gore-tex of Fort William's outdoor shops; and the Nevis gorge, which really is a shame to miss.

■ Follow the B8004 for 2 miles (3km), then branch right on a faint field track to Spean Bridge school. Take the small road S of the River Spean to

Corriechoille. Track leads SE to Lairig Leacach bothy.

■ Take the path on either side of Allt na Lairige to Loch Treig, then the track and swampy path to Corrour Station.

CORROUR TO DALWHINNIE

■ A track runs along the S side of Loch Ossian. The path up the Uisge Labhair goes further than the map thinks, to lose itself at a green meadow (GR 467726). Slant up to the stalkers' path above to pass through the Bealach Dubh (the Black Pass).

■ After Culra bothy keep to the left of Allt a' Chaoil-reidhe. Where tracks meet E of Loch Pattack (GR546789), go straight uphill to left of a new deer fence to a path at the 460m contour. Turn right along the path for 400yd/m to a gate. Turn uphill with fence on your left, and at the top of the plantation turn right for 200yd/m to a gate onto open hill.

■ 3 miles (5km) of ridge lead to the Fara's summit. Descend (compass-bearing) to a wide gap running down through trees from GR609837. A track

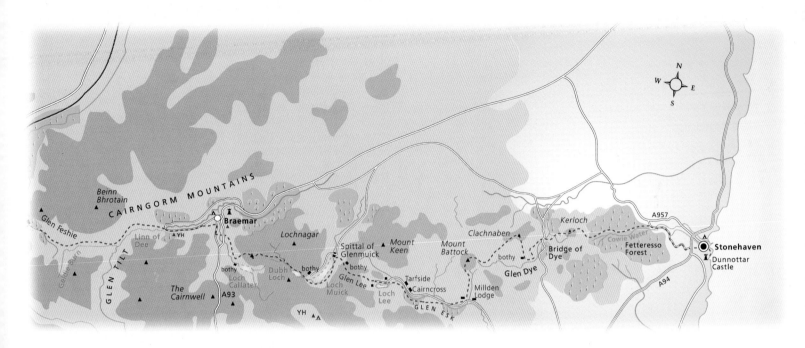

Key to Maps

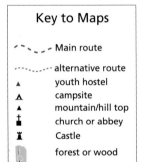

- – – – Main route
- ········ alternative route
- ▲ youth hostel
- △ campsite
- ▲ mountain/hill top
- ✝ church or abbey
- ⚏ Castle
- 🌳 forest or wood

leads out past the castle gatehouse to Dalwhinnie.

DALWHINNIE TO GLEN FESHIE

■ An aqueduct leads NE under the A9 to tracks that pass to S of Meall Chuaich. A small path zigzags up the steep headwall of Coire Chuaich. Head just S of E (in mist, on a careful compass bearing) towards the hump of Sgor Dearg. On the narrow neck leading to it will be found the stalkers' path down to Gaick Lodge.

■ The footbridge leading to Gaick Lodge is broken but there is a wide ford. Turn left after Gaick Lodge; ½ mile (800m) after the dam of Loch an t-Seilich take a faint path up right,

crossing eastwards to meet Allt Bhran. This is followed upstream.

■ At a stream junction after 2 miles (3km) (GR798886) turn N uphill, to pass up the left edge of a plantation to a track. Follow this NE to Glen Feshie. It's usually possible to wade the River Feshie; or there's a bridge 800yd/m downstream.

FESHIE TO BRAEMAR

■ A track leads gloriously upstream.

After 3½ miles (6km) the track turns away uphill towards a quarry; here the path runs ahead, keeping close to the river.

■ After 2 miles (3km), at a small tumbledown hut, slant up left to a footbridge over the River Eidart. The path turns downstream for 50yd/m, then left to descend gradually E. Near Geldie Lodge it joins a Landrover track that leads to Linn of Dee.

■ Take road towards Braemer. After 4

miles (7km), just before a car park on the left, a track on the right has a locked gate with ladder stile.

■ The main track slants uphill to a small pool. Keep E and slightly uphill across the complex junction above, to a ladder stile leading into the Morrone Birkwood (GR127902).

Paths through the heather converge onto a trodden track running E, and a descending lane into Braemar.

DISTANCE CHART (cumulative)

	MLS	KM	COMMENTS
Mallaig	0	0	
Inverie	0	0	bunkhouses
+Sourlies	9	14	bothy
Glen Dessarry	15	24	bothy A'Chuill
+Tomdoun	30	48	inn only
Achnacarry	45	72	Post Office only
Spean Bridge + 4mls			
SHORT CUT TO CORROUR			
Spean Bridge	51	82	
+Lairig Leacach	59	95	bothy
+Corrour	67	108	bunkhouse only
Glen Loy	50	80	hotel only
Fort William	56	90	YH
Luibeilt	69	111	bothy
Staoineag	71	114	bothy

	MLS	KM	COMMENTS
+Corrour	76	122	bunkhouse only
Loch Ossian	77	124	YH only
Culra	88	142	bothy
Dalwhinnie	97	156	shop at café, inns
+Glen Feshie	117	188	bothy
Inverey	134	216	YH only
Braemar	139	224	
Lochcallater	145	233	bothy
Glas-allt Shiel	152	246	bothy
+Shielin of Mark	158	254	bothy
Tarfside	170	274	shop has closed
+Charr	179	288	bothy (see note below)
Stonehaven	201	323	
Dunnottar	202	325	no facilities
+ indicates the Very Romantic Nightspots			

BRAEMAR TO MARK

■ Head S out of Braemar on the minor road to west of Clunie Water, to turn left after all fenced fields to a footbridge (GR154882). Track leads up Glen Callater. Just before Lochcallater Lodge a rough path climbs steeply to the left. High on Carn an t-Sagairt Mor it turns right to contour round the hill until it's running NE.

■ Remain on the path to cross two streams (GR217845). Slant down the valley of the Allt an Dubh-loch, keeping left of the bogs of the valley floor. Join the stream as the valley steepens and the Dubh Loch is seen.

■ Keep to left of the stream, to descend past the Dubh Loch. Turn right, around the head of Loch Muick, to Spittal of Glenmuick.

Turn up right between the buildings into a little ravine. Follow streams (rather than taking bearings across the peat hags). Note that Shielin of Mark is beside a small river running NE.

SHIELIN OF MARK TO CHARR

■ Head E downstream, then up a side stream still E, to find a Landrover track at the ridge of Muckle Cairn (GR354824). It leads down into Glen Lee and past Loch Lee to Invermark Castle. Now paths and tracks to south of the river run along Glen Esk. The Glenesk footbridges have been built by the Dalhousie Estate for its own use, and those who cross do so at their own risk.

■ From Corharncross, descend to a final footbridge and take a track over the shoulder of Craig Crane to Millden Lodge. Tracks run N into the hills: one up Hill of Turret is a short-cut to the head of Glen Dye. A better way is to take the left-hand track, which climbs most of the way up Mount Battock.

■ A new track starts near the summit of Mount Battock, descending E to join the one marked on the map. Fork right beside the Burn of Badymicks to Charr bothy.

CHARR TO DUNNOTTAR

■ Track N leads to the ridge just W of Clachnaben, with a peaty path and short scramble to the summit. A path descends E to track near Glendye Lodge. Do not turn right past the Lodge (private) but follow a rougher track ahead to meet the B974 800yd/m north of Bridge of Dye.

■ The path opposite features a missing footbridge (GR656869), so use the track to Heatheryhaugh. Old tracks run towards Kerloch, meeting a forest road. A path leaves the track to run over Kerloch itself.

■ At Glenskinnan is a puzzling junction (GR707888). A SRWS sign 'Glenbervie' indicates a rough track ahead into the open heather. This track bends right and then re-enters trees. A new forest road joins it – a green waymark of the SRWS points forward. The road descends then bends left, and another waymark indicates the old track continuing ahead to cross a stream (GR722876).

■ This pleasant sandy path runs beside a fence and bends left into taller trees. It becomes a forest road, then joins a much bigger, newer road. Here the SRWS sign points right, but we follow a mountain bike trail ahead.

■ After 3 miles (5km) at GR766877 is another confusing junction. The main track (which is not marked on the map) climbs N, away from the water: watch out here for a small old track forking right. This pleasanter track eventually escapes from the forest at Mergie.

■ A minor road runs to Cheyne Hill, where a driveway track on the left runs down to Kirktown of Fetteresso. A bridge over the A94 lets you into Stonehaven.

■ Keep ahead to the seafront and a dogwalking path to the old harbour. Before the Marine Hotel, turn into Wallace Wynd and left in Castle Street to find the start of the clifftop path.

■ The path joins a road above, then branches off on the left. The next section has been denigrated by Aberdeenshire as 'dangerous and unsuitable', and walkers must make their own minds up whether to divert onto the road.

■ Try to arrive at fascinating Dunnottar during normal office hours, as it is impregnable at other times.

ESSENTIAL INFORMATION

Start: Mallaig, for boat to Inverie
Finish: Stonehaven
Distance: 200 miles (320km)
Distance on roads: 20 miles (32km)
Total ascent: 17,000ft (5000m)
Time: 10 long days (of 20mls/32km and 1700ft/500m of ascent) to have a roof overhead every night. Moderately-paced walkers could take 14 days (of 14mls/23km) but will have to carry a tent
Terrain: Paths and tracks, but through remote mountain country and with many passes of 2000–3000ft (600–900m) altitude
Note: In summer 2000 Charr bothy was closed because of persistent vandalism. If it remains unavailable, a diversion may be needed to Feltercairn or Anchenblae

MAPS AND GUIDES

OS Landrangers Nos 33, 34, 41, 42, 43, 44 and 45
No guidebook to this specific route

TRANSPORT

Mallaig is served by the beautiful West Highland Line from Glasgow. Boat to Knoydart on Mon, Wed, Fri: Bruce Watt 01687 462320. Stonehaven has good rail and bus links with Edinburgh, Glasgow and the South. Fort William, Corrour and Dalwhinnie have railway stations. Braemar has bus links with Aberdeen only

ACCESS

East of Dalwhinnie the route is mostly not on recognised rights-of-way, so isn't suitable for use during the stalking season (mid-August to mid-October)

TOURIST INFORMATION

Fort William 01397 703781
Aberdeen 01224 632727
Stonehaven 01569 762806

right: Bothies are delightful, but unreliable. Meanach in Glen Nevis, under repair

Irish Sea to North Sea

Lakeland to Lindisfarne

Lakeland to Lindisfarne is a 190-mile (305km) coast-to-coast between Ravenglass and Holy Island, taking in the hills of the Lake District, the high Pennines and the Northumberland coast. The low-level Lakeland to Lindisfarne route is not a difficult one: it's about on a par with Wainwright's Coast-to-Coast and much easier than the Pennine Way. The mountain alternative route, though easier than Snowdonia to Gower or the Scottish Coast-to-Coasts, is tougher and would throw out a stiff navigational test to the inexperienced walker.

'A coast-to-coast across the Lake District and the Pennines to the North Sea? Wainwright's already done it,' I hear you say. But why should Wainwright have all the fun, steal all the best bits, and didn't he go wrong – just a tiny little bit – on the Cumbrian plains, the flatlands between the Yorkshire Dales and the North York Moors?

My route started life back in the eighties – as Ravenglass to Edinburgh, a 260-mile (416km) epic that left England at Kielder and crossed the Southern Uplands to Scotland's historic first city.

right: Lindisfarne Castle at sunrise. When high tides come in, Holy Island's tourists rush back to the mainland, leaving this magical place of saints and pilgrims to you

But instead of walking it I got married to Nicola, so Ravenglass to Edinburgh was forgotten; put into a dark drawer, somewhere in the loft.

Several years later, Nicola said that she'd like to do a long-distance route with me but she didn't want to do any of the camping on the tops that I had talked so enthusiastically about. We would do the walk in style: stay at B&Bs and eat bacon and eggs, not muesli and tea made with powdered milk. Oh! And Ravenglass to Edinburgh's 260 miles was too far.

Edinburgh would have to be dropped. Looking at the maps I found that we could come off the hills to one of those castles on the Northumberland coast. But which castle?

Bamburgh might be the place, and so could Dunstanburgh. But when you get to the coast you look across the waves to yet another castle – Lindisfarne on Holy Island. How romantic to be stranded for the night on the island colonised by the early Christians, Aidan and Cuthbert.

The in-between routes of the Lake District were easy. Muncaster Fell, the hill above Ravenglass, drops you nicely into Eskdale, and Eskdale's just one ridge away from Wasdale, Lakeland's most spectacular valley. The next couple of days explores the heart of the Lakes – you could pick from a dozen routes hereabouts. Beyond Ambleside you need to go northwest to find a good line across the flatlands of the Eden valley. Two ways work. For the original book I chose Kentmere and Haweswater (now an alternative for campers). I have since modified the

above: A tranquil scene on Ullswater, seen here from the eastern shoreline path, perhaps the finest low-level path in England

route to go by way of Patterdale and Ullswater. This offers a wider choice of accommodation for non-campers.

In Northumbria good paths were harder to find. Some were non-existent on the ground and not signposted: others were blocked by barbed wire. Many more were made unpleasant by the farmer's plough or by five-foot high oil-seed rape. Council footpath officers pleaded poverty when asked to reinstate the paths. We were on our own.

But bit by bit the route was pieced together, and we set out on our first crossing.

DAMP DAYS, DUCKS AND SILENT WORDS ON A COAST-TO-COAST WITHOUT WAINWRIGHT

Somewhere amongst that swirling grey mist are some of the Lake District's finest rocky peaks, though you wouldn't know it. And somewhere among those rocky peaks are England's only golden eagles: they're keeping a low profile too.

Nicola says nothing as we climb the tortuous boulder-ridden path that I told her was a splendid trek to the tops. She says nothing about my attempts to cajole her through the entire width of the English Lakes in three days on what is her first long-distance walk, and nothing about the incessant rain that trickles between our necks and our waterproofs. She says nothing, but I hear it all. After all I am a guide book writer. I invented this route, and I am the expert on what's fun in the mountains.

We press on; the rain presses on even harder, but the sting cannot match the pain of my embarrassment.

Three days ago we left Ravenglass on the Cumbrian coast to the sun and the seagulls. Within an hour of this take-it-easy sort of day we were strolling among the rocky bluffs and the wind-warped rowans of Muncaster Fell; by evening we had our feet up in the outside bar of the Wasdale Head Inn. Lingmell through a beer glass at twilight had never looked so good.

The next morning old packhorse trails took us into those high mountains before depositing us in yet another beer garden, this time at the Old Dungeon Ghyll Hotel, where we were entertained by musicians playing old Eagles songs.

Yes, this was the life!

Well, it would have been if I'd planned the day to end at five in Elterwater. But I planned it to end at Ambleside, and it was seven-thirty.

The next day saw Nicola limping among Wordsworth's daffodils, struggling through Skelghyll Woods, and hobbling up the rough Garburn Pass track. Had she battled with her injuries just to be here, in the dampness of Kentmere?

The rain still pours and our tortuous zigzag path reaches Nan Bield, a high

left: Great Gable and Sty Head Tarn feature early on the second day traverse between Wasdale and Langdale

above: Approaching Greg's Hut on the shoulder of Cross Fell. It's seen here under calm conditions quite unlike those experienced by John and Nicola

windswept pass hemmed in by crags. The rocks are shiny with water and so are we. Finding a wet rock away from the howling wind, I reach for the tea. It's amazing how good flask tea tastes when you're out in the open, considering how bad it tastes when you try to finish it off back home. If things were bad here, what would they be like in the Eden Valley, where the map promised only dull flatlands?

Well, the tea got Nicola talking, even if it was just to say her knees wouldn't bend and her feet were raw. We fumbled down the rocks to the shores of Haweswater. The plan was to walk the splendid paths along its western shores, but today they didn't seem too splendid, so we put on our nice soft trainers and walked down the lane instead.

After a very slow pint at the Haweswater Hotel we floated down, limbs anaesthetised, to Bampton Grange. Hanging over the bridge, we watched as some of the locals raced plastic ducks down the river – sensible folk on such a day. After the excitement of a close finish everybody traipsed into the Crown and Mitre, our B&B for the night.

We had always hoped for the best weather to be saved for the days spent on high ground but we got it on the next day, which was to be a short one. One little limestone hill and we were out of Lakeland. Basking in sunlight, we strolled across the pastures of Eden on country lanes and riverside paths, through villages with apple and cherry blossom … and into Mrs Jephcott's at Temple Sowerby.

Nicola needed mollycoddling after her hardships, and Mrs J was the person to do it. Tea and biscuits were waiting on our arrival – just the thing, as we'd had no lunch. Mrs J had taken Nicola's 'no lunch' remark of yesterday very seriously and provided a breakfast to last all day. Huge portions of scrambled egg accompanied the sizzling smoked bacon, mushrooms, fried bread and tomatoes.

It seemed a shame to leave the green fields of Eden, but Cross Fell had been casting its shadow across the fields for a while. We could see fluffy white cloud skimming over its summit. But those pretty clouds meant there was a Helm Wind, and a Helm Wind meant trouble. This wind builds its strength on the slopes of Hexhamshire Common then unleashes its full force over the edge of Cross Fell. Often walkers caught in Helm Winds are forced to their knees and unable to make further progress.

At Kirkland there's nowhere else to go but up. The winds strengthen and the clouds close in as we climb to the shoulder of the moor. We expect the worst, but suddenly there's quiet, there's total sunshine again and we can picnic on the top. Looking back across the chequered pastures of Eden we could see the Lakeland mountains in vivid detail – even the paths stood out.

A lead-miners' track takes the route through some of the remotest and complex hills in England, and it is with relief that we descend safely into the South Tyne Valley. In the George and Dragon at Garrigill, we traded stories with mud-stained Pennine Wayfarers. They talked of their adventures in the peat bogs of Kinder, and we of rocky mountain traverses and a sunset over Wastwater.

From Garrigill we climbed over a dark windswept moor and into the next valley at Nenthead. Today the old lead-mining village was closed, and dreary under the blanket of low grey cloud. A dull day in Nenthead keeps your expectations low and your feet on the ground. There's

above: Holm's Linn makes a pleasing contrast to the stark heather moors surrounding Allendale

left: Alnwick Castle and the sleepy River Aln

a Wright Brothers' garage, but these brothers don't fly aeroplanes: they drive buses. We climbed out of Nenthead past a blackened statue with railings round it, then out of Cumbria.

Northumberland greeted us with more driving rain as we reached the top of the Black Hill. A Ford Transit van pulled up beside us. 'Want a lift?' the driver asked. Nicola's face lit up for a moment, but I said, 'No thanks'. The white van disappeared into the murk, and we turned off the road onto a path ominously signposted the Black Way.

Everybody talks about blooming purple heather, but on a stormy day out of season, heather can be as dreary as the wet peat it grows in. Today its tangled stalks tried repeatedly to upend us whenever we lifted our eyes to the horizon. This must be England's bleakest moor.

East Allendale shyly presented itself. First as a sliver of green beneath the black, then as a pretty pastured valley with woodland hiding the fast-flowing river. Narrow paths squeezed through the woods to reveal a fine waterfall, Holm's Linn, and colourful wildflowers on steep grassy riverbanks.

But Northumberland had been as kind as it was going to be today. Raindrops regrouped on the sycamore leaves, then bucketed down our necks. By the time we reached Allendale Town we were drenched.

Allendale Town is really a village, even though its four-storey buildings suggest that it has known greater importance. Our hotel, the Heatherlea, looked posh, so we thought we had better take our muddy boots off at least.

'Hoody was here,' proclaimed the graffiti on the stone walls of the bus shelter. 'Well, he wouldn't want to be here now,' I thought as I watched the steam waft from my thick red walking socks. At the Heatherlea they gave us the bridal suite, which was nice – there was plenty of room to hang up our soggy clothes.

It's a short section – just ten miles to Hexham. Normally it would be a quick one, too, over the heather moors of Hexhamshire Common and down leafy lanes and woodland paths.

But today a little spice had been sprinkled into our itinerary. Nicola opened the bedroom curtains and wiped away the condensation on the windowpane.

'It's snowing!'

left: The summit of Harrison Stickle is seen on the mountain route, which continues along the Blea Rigg ridge, seen here to the left, above Great Langdale. The low-level route follows the valley floor (right)

With our boots and socks still damp from yesterday, we squelched up the lane into the grey and white murk of the hillside. Primroses poked through the snowflakes on the roadside verges. Through the top gate at the end of the road we could see that any semblance of a path was hidden under a blanket of snow. Here was my chance to regain expert status, something that sadly had been lost on the pretty paths of the Lake District. I did so by getting across safely on a compass bearing, only to lose the compass and credibility together somewhere on the streets of Alnwick.

Hexham's too fine a place not to dwell in. Its magnificent priory dominates the town centre; its Moot Hall and Manor House add to the market town's proud history.

North of Hexham we spent two more days in the rain. Sloshing through the fields of the North Tyne, and climbing through misty spruce forests, we could have done with wellingtons rather than walking boots. My boots were sad – and leaking: I'd asked of them one trip too many. Their reward was to be discarded in an Alnwick waste bin.

I remembered Alnwick from my misspent youth in bedsitter Newcastle. Like me, it had tidied itself up since then. A magnificent castle stands out from the town's Georgian terraces and cobbled ginnels. It's only 8 miles (13km) to the coast at Boulmer.

Socks and boots tossed off, and sand in her Elastoplast-covered toes, Nicola rushed for the crashing North Sea waves, and soaked herself in cool surf. She's always loved the sea. I was content to take in that salty air and search for seafood in the nearest rockpool.

The rugged Northumberland coastline transforms many times. The ruins of Dunstanburgh Castle, set on dark dramatic cliffs north of Craster, are followed by two rocky coves, Newton Haven and Football Hole. Then there's the long, sweeping sands of Beadnell Bay. Two fishing villages, Beadnell and Seahouses lie between here and Bamburgh. Beadnell's a rustic place with lime kilns on the seafront, while Seahouses is like a mini-Blackpool, with funhouses and ice-cream stalls. But then you're back to the rockpools, the sand and the kittiwakes.

The locals call it haar. Before we knew what was happening, this swirling mist had drifted in from the sea, and made mysterious shadows of all around us. Small rocks could have been cliffs, and headlands mere rocky islets. Wanting to keep our toes sand-free we had been keeping to the east of the dunes. In doing so we nearly missed Bamburgh Castle and a well-earned cup of tea at the local café.

The red sandstone fortress is not as romantic as some, having been modernised many times. People live here in double-glazed luxury. But Bamburgh's sheer scale cannot fail to impress. From rocky perches it towers over the beach and the village green.

We arrived at Beal Sands. The timetable said that we had enough time to cross safely to Holy Island. A line of poles marked the ancient Pilgrims' Route, but those sands looked more like mud; deep, deep, 'you'll sink to the bottom if you dare tread on me' type mud. I used the excuse that we didn't want to be treading all that mud into our nice B&B. Nicola nodded and we followed the easy tarmac causeway instead.

Free of heavy backpacks but filled with tea and scones, we walked the shoreline, passing a little chapel, then some fishing boats. The tide came lapping back onto the sands: the noisy seagulls came with it. In silence we watched the setting sun flickering pink onto the grey North Sea waves and flooding red into the skies behind the castle walls.

right: Bamburgh Castle in silvery morning light. It's one of the many impressive fortresses seen on routes through Northumberland

Lakeland to Lindisfarne: The Route

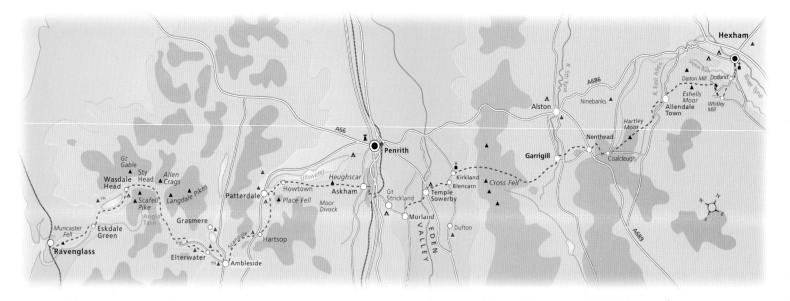

RAVENGLASS TO WASDALE HEAD

▨ Start through the woods of Walls Plantation, past the ruins of the Roman bath house (Walls Castle) to join the A595 by Home Farm (GR096966). A track, Fell Lane, climbs NE over Muncaster Fell.

▨ At the other end of the fell, a bridleway descends N past Irton Green Station. Here, a lane leads to the road W of Eskdale Green.

▨ Go through the village, beyond a lake, then follow a walled track past Low Holme Farm. Across a tarmac lane, a bridleway crosses a stone bridge over the River Mite, before climbing through mixed woodland to Irton Fell.

▨ A fine ridgewalk now follows, over the summits of Whin Rigg, then Illgill Head, close to the edge of some cliffs that plummet 1500 feet (500m) into Wastwater. The day ends with a splendid descent to the shores of Wastwater into Wasdale Head.

WASDALE HEAD TO LANGDALE

▨ Today's route takes you into spectacular mountainscapes over trails, once trodden by smugglers and the hooves of their Galloway ponies. It climbs out of Wasdale beneath Great Gable's scree slopes to reach Sty Head. From here it heads SW, climbing beneath the cliffs of Great End to Sprinkling Tarn,

then onwards in a corridor of crag to Angle Tarn.

▨ Beyond the tarn there's a short climb to the col beneath the crags of Bowfell. Here you look down a stony chasm, Rossett Gill, into a bare valley, Mickleden. A stony track avoids the gill by zigzagging down the hillside to the right.

▨ The track enters Langdale, passing both the Old and New Dungeon Ghyll Hotels to reach the main road. Turn right along the road for 200yd/m, then left along the drive to Side House. Here a path continues E beneath the slopes of Lingmoor and into Chapel Stile.

▨ Follow the road for a short way past the Wainwright Hotel before turning right

to cross Great Langdale Beck. The path traces the beck into Elterwater.

LANGDALE TO PATTERDALE

▨ From Elterwater, you round Loughrigg Tarn, follow the bridleway round the skirt of Ivy Crag, then continue E over the shoulder of Loughrigg Fell into bustling Ambleside.

▨ Head N out of Ambleside, taking the track past High Sweden Bridge to the Scandale Pass. Descend by a little stream past Hartsop Hall and its pleasant woods to the shores of Brotherswater, and the road at Cow Bridge (GR403134).

▨ For the best way into Patterdale, turn right, then left almost into Hartsop

village, then turn left again up a narrow tarmac lane/track heading N into Patterdale.

PATTERDALE TO ASKHAM

▨ Today's route alongside the eastern shores of Ullswater is the finest stretch of low-level path in England. The bridleway, joined at Side Farm, passes beneath the crags and screes of Place Fell, dodging rowans, pines and aromatic juniper in an undulating course round headlands to the hamlet of Sandwick. Here, soft green valleys delve into Martindale's steep fellsides of bracken.

▨ Beyond the Howtown Inn the route climbs past Mellguards Farm before raking across the sides of Arthur's Pike to reach Moor Divock, stark high ground with a Roman road and the settlements of ancient Britons.

▨ Near the limestone outcrops of Heughscar Hill, a wide grassy track takes the route into Askham, a picturesque village with expansive village greens.

ASKHAM TO TEMPLE SOWERBY

▨ Head S on a track tracing the east bank of the River Lowther. At Whale Farm turn left along a tarmac lane that winds among fields of the Lowther Estate.

left: High Sweden Bridge, north of Ambleside

Turn left on reaching the bridleway from High Knipe, which climbs alongside a pine plantation, then swings N to meet an estate road at GR541219. A leatside bridleway now crosses a narrow wedge of woodland before going under the M6 motorway to the A6.

There's a short stretch N along the A-road, then some more tarmac on quiet country lanes through Great Strickland and Moreland.

Take the Cliburn road out of Moreland for about 600yd/m, then turn right along a bridleway by Moreland Beck. After passing Winter House and crossing the River Lyvannet, it emerges at the roadside by Crossrigg Hall. Country lanes lead to Ousenstand Bridge, where a footpath follows the NE bank of the River Eden to Temple Sowerby.

TEMPLE SOWERBY TO GARRIGILL

A little footpath signposted to the Newbiggin Road heads NE from the back of the village green. A path staggered to the left along the lane passes Acorn Bank, now owned by the National Trust but once colonised by the Knight's Templar.

Under a railway viaduct, the path follows Syke Beck to the outskirts of Newbiggin, where quiet lanes with high hedges lead past Blencarn into Kirkland.

Leave the village on a lane that soon becomes a track climbing the slopes of Cross Fell.

The track straddles the bleak moorland ridge north of Cross Fell, passing Greg's Hut and the old lead mines, before making a long descent into Garrigill.

GARRIGILL TO ALLENDALE TOWN

From the village green take the farm track climbing out of the valley, past Loaning Head and up to the Middleton-in-Teesdale road. Turn left along the road to Garrigill Burn (GR751424). Trace the streamside path uphill beyond the old Bentyfield mines, then climb NE over rough pastures. The path rounds the forest at GR772437 (not cutting a corner through it as the maps show), then descends to Nenthead.

Take the road climbing towards Whitehall, then the walled track E to the summit of Black Hill, where the Allenheads road is met. You're now in Northumberland.

Turn left along the high road past Coalcleugh, then head NE along the bridleway traversing the heather of Carrshield Moor to reach a high moorland lane near Knockshield. Follow lanes to GR845523, where a footpath descends to the River East Allen's east bank, then crosses a footbridge beyond the attractive Holmes Linn falls.

The route continues along a path over rolling pasture on the west side of the river. After recrossing the river at GR838545 near Peckriding, it climbs to the B-road just half a mile short of Allendale Town.

ALLENDALE TOWN TO HEXHAM

Take the lanes up to Moorhouse Gate. Here a green track continues E across Eshells Moor, which is part of the vast heather uplands of Hexhamshire Common.

At High Eshells Farm more country lanes lead down past Dalton to Whitley Mill GR924603. A footpath by a ford heads N, crosses Ham Burn, then climbs past the conifers of Dotland Grange to reach the road by Dotland Farm (the site of a medieval village).

Follow the lane from Dotland into the little valley of Dipton Burn. The ivy-clad pub, Dipton Mill, is one of the nicest on the journey and serves bar meals in a beer garden at the back.

Turn right on a path past some stables to Hole House. The path swings N squeezing past the cottage, through a wood, then across fields at Queens Letch. Letch once meant a slip and it was here, during the Wars of the Roses, that Queen Margaret was said to have fallen from her horse while making her escape to France.

After crossing a minor road the path descends across fields into Hexham.

HEXHAM TO WEST WOODBURN

Today's complex route leaves Hexham N across the Tyne road bridge. A tarmac lane (L) takes the route over the A69, then uphill to The Riding, where a path descends into a wooded dene before climbing out to the village of Acomb.

At GR932665, past the two village pubs, a track (R) heads N across fields, back to the road at Halfway House, then across more fields to rejoin the road south of Hill Head. Cross the line of Hadrian's Wall (the stonework

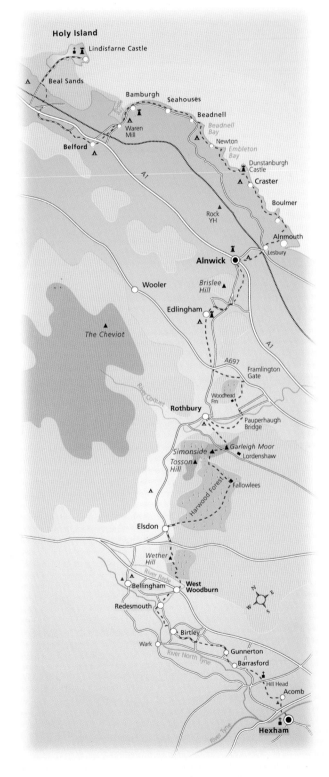

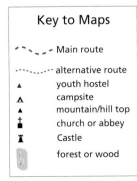

Key to Maps

- – – – – Main route
- ·········· alternative route
- ▲ youth hostel
- ⚊ campsite
- ▲ mountain/hill top
- ✝ church or abbey
- ♟ Castle
- 🌲 forest or wood

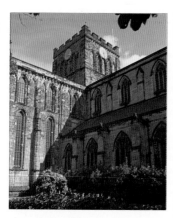

above: Hexham Abbey

has long been dismantled). The tall wooden cross here was erected to commemorate the Battle of Heavenfield where Christian King Oswald defeated the Celtic warlord, Cadwalla.

■ After passing the little chapel of St Oswald's, the path traverses undulating hill pastures, before descending left of an old quarry to the road near Chollerton.

■ Lanes now take the route through Barrasford, where there's an excellent pub for bar food. Beyond the village a path skirts the nearside of Barrasford Quarry at GR909741, and crosses fields into Gunnerton. Here, take the Birtley lane NW before turning off left across fields and by Mallow Burn. Another stretch of country lane beyond Pit House is followed by a field path into Birtley village.

■ Follow lanes N out of Birtley to GR878790, before descending NW across rough pastureland to cross Holywell Burn. The path then threads between two woods before joining a lane above Heugh Farm and Countesspark Woods.

■ At a sharp bend the lane should be abandoned for a path descending meadowland to the River North Tyne. The path traces the riverbank through the woods before climbing right to join the old railway trackbed. This leads into Redesmouth, passing close to the old railway station.

■ Take the Bellingham road over Redesmouth Bridge, turn right on a vehicle track signposted 'Border County Ride', then left along a green lane to Hole Farm on the West Woodburn road. Follow the road into West Woodburn.

WEST WOODBURN TO ROTHBURY

■ Leave the Town Head road at GR898872 for a path aiming NW across fields to the footbridge over the River Rede. Across the river, turn left on a dirt path beneath some woods.

■ Beyond a footbridge the route climbs N to meet the road and a spruce plantation on the skyline. After turning right along the road for 500yd/m climb N, following a waymarked footpath through the trees and onto the summit trig point of Whether Hill.

■ The path now descends into Upper Redesdale and the busy A696 at Raylees. Across the main road, follow the narrow lane over a hill and down into Elsdon. This pleasing village has wide greens, a little church, a fine pub and a farmhouse with an intact pele tower.

■ Take the road out of Elsdon W past Landshott and into Harwood Forest. Just by Whitlees Farm, a waymarked footpath climbs through the trees to Manside Cross where the earthworks of an ancient fort lie next to the plinth of a collapsed cross.

■ About 800yd/m E of the cross the route meets a forestry track. Flinted tracks now take a circuitous route past Redpath and Fallowlees farms to the edge of the Simonside heather moors (GR020964).

■ There's a trackless course N past the rock outcrop of Selby's Cove to the col W of Simonside. Here a well-worn path climbs to the rocky summit where you

look out across most of Northumberland, including the big Cheviots, the green fields of the Coquet Valley and the pale blue strip that is the North Sea.

■ The prominent path continues E across subsidiary tops, finally descending Garleigh Moor to Whitton on the outskirts of Rothbury.

ROTHBURY TO ALNWICK

■ The Coquet is a fine river to follow, even if it's not going in the perfect direction for our route. Lakeland to Lindisfarne takes to the lanes parallel to the S bank before following an old railway trackbed past Wagtail Farm. Leave the trackbed at a step-stile on the left for a path, then a farm track past Craghead cottage (not on Landranger map) and West Farm. Turn left at the crossroads of tracks to pass the front of another farmhouse, before descending back to the Coquet at Pauperhaugh Bridge.

■ After turning right along the road, go left (N) and follow the road, then the track past Woodhead Farm (GR105015). Beyond the farm climb left on the bridleway to the corner of some woods, then turn right along the green road that skirts the foot of open moor. The continuing path through the conifers of Lonframlington Common is impassable so take the bridleway on the right to the A697, follow the road for about 600yd/m to Framlington Gate, then fork left on a wide track to the

crossroads near New Moor House.

■ Just beyond the crossroads on the A697 take the path N to Wandeysteads and cross Long Plantation to join the muddy farm track that leads past Demesne Farm into Edlingham. This isolated village has a ruined thirteenth-century castle and a fine stone-built railway viaduct, now disused.

■ From the church, follow the footpath signposted 'Lemmington Hall', passing the castle and descending to some woods. Through the woods and across Edlingham Burn the path climbs to Overthwarts Farm and traces its drive to the road, which leads right to the B6341.

■ Follow this for 800yd/m to the crossroads at Banktop, turn right, then left near Hadwins Close Farm. A footpath on the right (GR157106), signposted 'Half Crown Well and Intake', heads NE across fields and crosses the old railway before joining a track to Intake Farm and the road.

■ Follow the road N for 300yd/m, then turn right along a track skirting Swansfield Park Golf Course. Turn left along a tarmac lane beyond the clubhouse, but leave it at a right-hand bend for a narrow walled track that descends to Alnwick.

ALNWICK TO BEADNELL

■ South of the Bondgate Tower, take the B1340 signposted to Bamburgh before turning right on a pedestrianised lane past a new housing estate

DISTANCE CHART (cumulative)

	MLS	KM	COMMENTS		MLS	KM	COMMENTS
Ravenglass	0	0	shops, hotel, inns B&Bs	Acomb	95	153	inn, YH only
Eskdale Green	6	10	shops, hotel, inns, B&Bs	Barrasford	102	164	inn
Nether Wasdale	9	14	inns and YH only	West Woodburn	114	183	inns (YH at Bellingham)
Wasdale Head	14	23	inn, B&B, campsite,	Elsdon	120	193	pub
Old Dungeon Gill Hotel	21	34	inn, shop at campsite	Rothbury	133	214	shops, hotels, inns, B&Bs
Elterwater	25	40	shop, inn, B&B, YH				
Ambleside	28	45	shops, hotels, inns, B&Bs, YH	Edlingham	144	232	campsite only
				Alnwick	151	243	shops, hotels, inns, B&Bs
Patterdale	37	60	shop, hotels, inns, B&Bs, YH	Boulmer	159	256	pub only
				Craster	162	261	pub, inn, shop
Askham	46	74	shop, inns only	Beadnell	169	272	hotels, B&Bs, shops
Morland	55	88	pubs only	Seahouses	171	275	hotels, inns, B&Bs, shops
Temple Sowerby	59	95	inn, shop only				
Kirkland	63	101		Bamburgh	175	282	hotel, B&Bs, campsite, shops
Garrigill	71	114	inn, shop, B&B				
Nenthead	74	119	inn, B&B, shop	Belford	180	290	hotel, B&Bs, shops
Allendale Town	84	135	hotels, inns, B&Bs, shops	Holy Island (village)	192	309	hotel, inns, B&Bs
Hexham	94	151	hotels, inns, B&Bs, shops				

(GR193132) then across fields. After turning right along a cart track, the route joins the A1068 for a short way before turning off (R) near Alndyke Farm to descend to the River Aln. Riverside paths now lead into Lesbury.

■ Follow the road through the village then take the Boulmer road. A signpost between cottages on the right shows the route across fields north of the Aln.

■ The path finally climbs to the road opposite the entrance to Foxton Hall and the golf club. The route to the seashore follows the drive and comes out by the Marden Rocks.

■ You've now done a coast-to-coast but there's lots more to come. Boulmer has a pub for those who want to celebrate, then there's Craster, renowned far and wide for its secret-recipe kippers.

■ Beyond Craster the route passes left of the fascinating ruins of Dunstanburgh Castle, famous for its connections with John of Gaunt and Henry V. Cross one of Northumberland's fine long beaches, Embleton Bay, before exploring two rocky coves, Newton Haven and Football Hole. The next long beach, Beadnell Bay, has sand dunes and a bird sanctuary. Beadnell village at the far end has plenty of B&Bs and a good inn for bar meals.

BEADNELL TO BELFORD

■ The shoreline route out of Beadnell is eventually forced back to the road by Annstead Burn on the outskirts of Seahouses. This large village has a strange mix of Blackpool-type amusement parlours and a Cornish-style harbour.

■ On the way out the route explores yet more rock pools and more sand dunes before reaching Bamburgh. Bamburgh Castle first appears across a vast area of tall sand dunes. You could walk straight past it without getting the soft sand of the dunes in your toes, but it would be a shame not to get a close-up of the magnificent sandstone fortress and the little village that lies behind.

■ Beyond Bamburgh you're confronted by the sands of Budle Bay. Although it looks easy to cross, do not try. There's a very fast-flowing channel in the middle and it has claimed quite a few lives. Instead, turn left with the shoreline to Kiln Point. Go left along the track here to avoid the deep mud of the inner bay.

■ A quiet lane then takes the route to Waren Mill, where a path continues W above the wooded Chesterhill Dean. On

reaching the next lane, turn left along it, then right along a field-edge W beneath a rocky outcrop known as Long Hills (not named on Landrangers). This path first crosses a railway siding, then the main Kings Cross to Edinburgh line (take care) before coming to the busy A1. On the other side of the road, a footpath crosses fields by a golf driving range to reach Belford.

■ Unless you're been lucky with the tide timetables, you'll be looking for a B&B. Belford has more of them than the rest of the area.

BELFORD TO HOLY ISLAND

Leave Belford past the Bluebell Inn on the road to Wooler, then turn right along an unsurfaced lane, passing Westhall and Craggyhall.

■ A path continues NW beneath a rocky hill, Chapel Crag, then into some woods. A wide forestry track then turns left to meet the lane E of Swinhoe Farm. Turn left along this then right, following the path N across fields to Detchant. Here a long, straight country lane continues NW past East Kyloe and Fenwick to meet the A1 again.

■ A lane across the busy road leads past Fenwick Granary, beyond which a tree-lined track continues for a short way to the Fenhamhill lane. Turn right along

this for a couple of hundred metres, then follow the path across cereal fields, over the railway track again, to reach the shoreline at Beal Sands.

■ Turn left, passing the concrete cube sea defences, to the causeway that crosses to Holy Island. Recheck with the tide timetables, and take no chances.

ESSENTIAL INFORMATION

Start: Ravenglass
Finish: Holy Island
Distance: 192mls/309km
Total Ascent: 45,000ft (15,000m)
Time: 11–14 days
Terrain: Low-level route: good paths over mountain passes of Lakeland; remote Pennine moorland, field and riverside paths through Northumberland, followed by easy coastal paths

MAPS AND GUIDES

OS Landranger 1:50 000 Nos 89, 90, 91, 87, 80, 81 and 75
Useful Outdoor Leisure Maps (1:25 000) that cover some of the route are Nos 5, 6, 7 and 31. These would replace Landrangers 89 and 90

Walking Lakeland to Lindisfarne by John Gillham (Grey Stone Books)
Lakeland to Lindisfarne by John Gillham (Crowood – out of print)

above: Approaching Dunstanburgh Castle from Craster

TRANSPORT

Ravenglass is served by British Rail and can be reached via Barrow or Carlisle. There is a bus off Holy Island stopping at the A1 at Beal. You can get another bus to Newcastle or Berwick from here. Both are on the London Kings Cross to Edinburgh railway line.
For those who want to get to the North West, trains run from Newcastle direct to Manchester, Liverpool and Carlisle

TIDE TIMETABLES

The Holy Island crossing timetables are essential for Lakeland to Lindisfarne. They can be obtained from the Tourist Information Centre at The Shambles, Alnwick, Northumberland NE66 1TN 01665 510665

TOURIST INFORMATION CENTRES

(Year-round opening)
Whitehaven 01946 852939
Ambleside 01539 432582
Penrith 01768 867466
   01434 605225
Alnwick 01665 510665
Berwick 01289 330733

North Sea to Atlantic
Beauly to Applecross

below: A single ridge of seven Munros and three Corbetts crosses Scotland from the Beauly Firth to Loch Carron. Its 30 high-level miles (50km) occupy the first three days of the walk. Here it rises towards its fifth mountain on the ridge of Craig Ghorm a' Bhealaich

The expedition to the Far North doesn't have to involve dog-sledges and light aircraft, and polar bears trying to pinch the pemmican. You can get the wild wastes, the fussing over supply dumps, the loneliness, self-reliance and anxiety, no further away than the northern tip of our own United Kingdom. Scotland's arctic has certain advantages over the proper Arctic: it's a lot cheaper to get to; it has real rocks and mountains to climb over instead of flat ice and the odd pressure ridge. It has – very occasionally, it's true – a warm place with beer in. And you don't have to carry any frozen seal meat at all if you don't want to.

There's no point in not carrying seal meat unless you've a worthwhile place not to carry it to. Scotland north of Inverness is, in coast-to-coast terms, serious – and seriously good. The mountains are big craggy ones, and they go all the way across. There's no need to find excitement in some bleak moor, or link along the forest tracks, or console yourself with alcohol along the roads of the eastern seaboard. This is the concentrated coast-to-coast. A full crossing of Highland and Grampian takes a fortnight. North of Inverness you get just as much mountain ground crammed into a single week.

Up in the Far North the mountains range from the good (Ben Wyvis, the Fannichs) to the outstanding (the Great Wilderness, Liathach, Inverpolly.) Ten of them lie side by side to form a single ridge that stretches across Scotland from the North Sea to Loch Carron. That ridge is the idea behind this chapter's walk. It's an idea that can't be realised in practice. For how can you stop at Strathcarron, when the high spiky hills of Achnashellach are dangling along the north-western horizon?

So we think again, and come up with the journey from B to A. Beauly, at the head of the Moray Firth, is as far inland as you can get and still be tidal. While Applecross, in the utmost west, lets you walk coast-to-coast while still being on the correct, western, side of Scotland almost all the time.

above: Maol Chean-dearg and Loch an Eion. The second half of the route wanders over – or among – these spiky Achnashellach hills

DAY ZERO

Beauly Priory is made of the Permian sandstone, which is much younger than the Old Red Sandstone, itself about a third of the age of the Torridonian that we'll finish the trip on. Still, it's a neat correspondence of geology. There's no roof on the priory, and the rain falls straight onto the stone tombs and makes grey reflections among the lettering. The place was built by civilising monks of, it says in Latin on the interpretation board, the Cabbage Hills. But the lands ahead are not civilised; the hills we're heading for are not cabbage hills.

We climbed the forest road to where the clouds brushed the pine-tips. Here are dreich reservoirs. Solitary pines dripped into black heather. We set the tent in a slightly less squelchy place below the dam.

DAY ONE

The first hills are ordinary, below a plain grey sky. Little paths through the heather lead to heather without little paths, and a long stony track with glimpses of a distant reservoir. Ahead, in the west, hills are more pointed. But first, we had to test our fitness against some eastern heather.

Now, I've told John that Scotland's going to be better than any of his walks across Wales. John, who's very keen on his Wales, hasn't quite believed me; and this deep, steep heather is rather proving his point. After 2000ft of a sort of lightfoot prancing about to give the impression that the heather isn't all that deep really, I get a bit embarrassed …. The onward walk is over 2000ft (600m) moorland, which is above the horrid heather and has, as a surprise bonus, an ancient stalking path not on the map. Things steepened, and we climbed alongside a sharp scarp. We were higher now, and beyond the next ridge further ridges were lifting themselves into the view: and not a road for two days, down towards the Cluanie Inn. 'This is better,' says John, 'quite like the Carneddau.'

At the top of a stiffish 500ft (150m) climb, John confronts, with mixed emotions, the cairn of his very first Munro. The twinkling hoar-frost on the cairn is particularly pretty, with its background of sleepy mountains tucking themselves up under a pink-and-green fluffy sunset. But this is May, not really the month for twinkling hoar-frost, and we're just about to tuck ourselves up under no fluffy blankets at all. We drop to the col and find a horizontal grass-bottomed hag at 2500ft (750m) for the tent.

DAY TWO

The remaining three of the Strathfarrar Four are standard middle-of-the-range Munros: no great crags, just a ridge that's sharp enough to see down both sides, and 2000ft (600m) of sides to see down, and rather rocky down one of them. The ridge swoops down 500ft (150m), and up 500 feet, and indeed is going to swoop up and down all the way to the West Coast.

Heading west it gets progressively more exciting, but the disadvantage is the weather in your face. So it's not fair that the weather's doing it backwards like us, and the sharp little snow showers are rushing up from behind and expending themselves on our rather large rucksacks. In a snow shower, it's not altogether easy to find the ridgeline off Sgurr a' Choire Ghlais, and we wander onto a little boulderfield. Stumbling over boulders in the snow reminds me of somewhere. Bleak boulders, empty grass, and a cold hand on the compass – no, of course it doesn't remind me of the Carneddau.

The ridge runs down off the Four onto rocky moorland, rubbed down by glacier to bare rock so it's good going as well as good geography. And behind it, a Corbett called An Sidhean: a 'Fairy Hill'. The top of it's a green lawn, but Gaelic fairies don't go in for dancing in rings on the grass. They prefer nastier games. The nearby cairn vanishes behind a hummock, and by the time we've walked far enough to have reached it three times over it's still not there. At last we discover it somewhere else entirely. And this is on an afternoon that's turning sunny; the trick would be just too easy in mist.

The sunniness increases as we drop into a peaty, stony glen with

right: Fuar Tholl – the name means Cold Hole – seen at dawn from a tent on Sgorr Ruadh

previous page: The low-level
route out along Gleann
Fhiodhaig. The 'fearsome
peat' turns out to be a
pleasant grassy riverbank.
The River Meig spreads wide
to reflect Creag Dubh Mhor,
and also to provide a
conveniently shingly and
shallow crossing-place. Heavy
rain makes such river-
crossings impossible, and
may impose a detour of hours
or even days

a tinkling stream. Here we decide not to go up the 1000ft (300m) of stimulating heather to the romantic lochan. Instead we take off our rucksacks and stop. Those rucksacks are heavy with unaccustomed luxuries, such as a tent, Karrimats, a stove and food not altogether artificial. What's the use of luxuries if you don't spend the evening wallowing in them? So we do that.

DAY THREE

The trouble with starting on middling mountains and then just getting better and better is this: if you stop halfway you miss out on all that better and better. John had sore feet and wanted to walk out over the peat hags. We had two maps, so that was OK.

I set out over the better and better. Maoile Lunndaidh is a sprawling lump, but it has a long corrie in its northern side, plus rocks, lochans and craggy sides. I looked down the corrie like a telescope to see a short bit of Gleann Fhiodhaig – along which poor John was at that moment plodding. John, as I learned later, had been feeling sorry for me in my deep heather ....

There was no porridge, and Ronald wasn't the type of Scotsman to hang about for a full English breakfast. Through the steam from my coffee-cup I watched him inch up Maoile Lunndaidh's immense heather slopes. If he'd looked back (he didn't – the poor chap seems to actually enjoy heather slopes) he'd have seen me disappear into the peat hags in search of the stalkers' path.

I'd been learning fast about this Scotland lark – too fast, as far as my feet were concerned – but not fast enough to do the bagful of Munros and the thousands of feet of ascent Ronald had planned for today. So I was taking the low route out to Achnashellach.

Stalkers obviously don't make big paths here, but eventually I managed to find a narrow track sneaking away among the heather. I followed it beside the cascades of the Allt an Amise and into a heathery ravine.

Down in Gleann Fhiodhaig, the Meig was waiting to introduce me to the art of Scottish river crossings: the grassy Landrover track was on the other bank, as was a herd of deer, the first I had ever seen. Even when I splashed out onto the northern bank, they just carried on grazing.

'No danger, it's only a Sassenach,' I could hear them thinking.

I put my wrinkled, blistered feet into some nice dry trainers and set off down the long valley.

So far on this journey rock scenery had been scarce. I had even dared to say that these northern Munros reminded me of the Carneddau. I did mention that the interesting mossy tops weren't quite the same as the Carneddau grasses but that wasn't enough. Ronald thinks most mountains south of the border are rather pathetic.

But as I rounded the corner beneath Sgurr nan Ceannaichean, I was confronted with some of the most spectacular peaks I have ever seen. The map named them as Fuar Tholl, Sgorr Ruadh and Beinn Liath Mhor. High above the drab moorland, sandstone glowed pink in the afternoon sun, with the vertical gullies and clefts as etched black shadows.

The view got more exciting with each step down the rough, now stony track, but unfortunately each step was aggravating my battered and unruly feet. As I walked under the aroma-therapeutic pine trees of Achnashellach I followed imaginary lines through those peaks – through to the imagined coast of Applecross. My mind was already halfway across. It was just my feet that weren't prepared to take me there ....

There's no need to feel sorry for anyone walking right across Scotland. Well, perhaps for the poor lost souls on Rannoch Moor – but not for John in his supposedly peaty valley, or me on my heather. Maoile Lunndaidh may be a broad lump, but it's a lump of pebbles and squishy moss: and maybe you can see a hundred mountains from Plynlimon, but not one of those is Bidean a' Choire Sheasgaich. (Ah, Sheasgaich! The dream-mountain of the Moinian Schist: pointy-topped, craggy-sided, sea-viewing, and even the saying of it as enjoyable as a well-executed sneeze. Scotland is never-ending because every hill you go up, you see another hill you want to go up even more. The long ridge runs onward; the Achnashellach spiky ones beckon from the north-west; down in Glen Carron the invisible hostel sings its seduction of hot water and soap and dry places to sit down on. So it's back next year for Sheasgaich, and after Sheasgaich its sharp-edged neighbour Lurg Mhor, and another long ridge eastwards. And before we know it we're on the ferry across Loch Ness, with our toes pointing at the Cairngorms and through to the North Sea ....)

Sgurr a' Chaorachain and Sgurr Choinnich, the Peak of Rowans and the Mossy Peak, sound unpromisingly vegetative, but you can't believe everything you hear. The Rowan one presents a

above: Sgurr Choinnich is the final Munro on the 30-mile (50km) ridge across Scotland

face of rock and grass. Still, these are friendly mid-Scotland mountains. The grass forms soft hollows all the way up through the rocks, until a little crest leads onto the ridge. The ridge is stony, and sharp, and swoops up over the Rowan one and down into a rocky gap and up the Mossy one.

There were people on the Mossy, the first met since the North Sea. They'd seen me on the ridge below, with my rather large pack, going up and then down, and thought I might be a parapentist preparing to hurl myself off some convenient crag. We discuss just how many mountains we're looking at. We start in the south-west – there's the Cuillin, that's nine to start with – but get distracted by distant skyline squiggles beyond An Teallach. Can it be the hills of Coigach? It can indeed.

Another human being is unfolding his tent in the Bealach Bhearnais. He doesn't know where he's going, but he's got maps down to Knoydart. And all night tonight he'll be looking along golden sea-lochs to Skye. Meanwhile I climb a final Corbett to find a well-built stalkers' path, from which I look not only out to Skye, but down shafts of late sun into the deep hollows of the Achnashellach hills. Backlit birches are like green flames as I drop into darkening Strath Carron.

DAY FOUR

Now things change. The rocks are no longer what hillwalkers call 'ordinary grey' but dirty white quartzite with an evil gleam, and dripping purple Torridonian. The hills aren't friendly, but go out of their way to be rather nasty. They have 1000ft drops between and no ridges.

The sensible thing would be to take the stalkers' path. The wonderful Bealach na Lice crossing dodges from the Strathcarron side to the Torridon side and back again as if dancing Strip the Willow. It then does a quick *pas-de-bas* round the cragbound Loch an Eoin before wandering down past the waterfalls to the Ben Damph Lodge for a malt whisky.

But I'm going over the mountains, and first off's Fuar Tholl, which doesn't mean mossy or rowan trees or anything nice like that. Fuar Tholl is 'Cold Hole' and be damned to you! Fuar Tholl has the famous Mainreachan Buttress which despite being vertical for much of its 800ft (250m), provides rockclimbing on surprisingly sound sandstone. The sandstone's sound because all the loose bits have dropped off to form the scree you climb up if you take the dramatic route up Fuar Tholl alongside its famous Mainreachan Buttress.

Then comes the plateau with the knolls and the little lochans. You go over a knoll and find one of the little lochans is – surprise – right in

left: Descending Maoile Lunndaidh on the third day. The intimidating slope of Beinn an Eion opposite turns out easier than it looks

front of you. So you go round the little lochan, and up the next knoll, and guess what? Another little lochan.

This is all good fun, but the top of Sgorr Ruadh (Red Craggy Thing) is simply good. Skye and sea-lochs, Liathach and An Teallach, the other spiky ones of Achnashellach clustered round their cragged loch, and a rocky sandstone ridge to start off down: the day may be grey but it's not snowing, not even looking like snow: what more can the humble hillwalker desire?

Well, he desires to get up the next Achnashellach spiky one, which is Maol Chean-dearg (Baldy Red-head). The bald red-head presents a very steep face, but there does seem to be a grassy rake up through the rocky bits, and that gully at the top's eroded so presumably it's been climbed. Indeed, there are a couple of people up there, though it's funny they should be moving quite so slowly.

Humans feel happier following in each other's footsteps. If the footsteps lead over a cliff, well, at least you aren't going over a cliff alone. And after 1000ft (300m) up the grassy rake, it would be tiresome to turn back just because the gully's a horrible stoneshoot of loose boulders and earth. If a pile of rock and dirt's sufficiently stable not to fall down off the mountain, then presumably so is a pile of rock and dirt with a hillwalker on top. And in the event, it doesn't. (I went back later and found a better way, by the eastern spur.)

An Ruadh-stac (the Red Heap) is another joke name, as it's made of evil-gleaming grey quartzite. You skirt a couple of green lochans and walk up 300ft (100m) of bare rock. Further up, the mountain softens a little and offers some scree and boulderfield sprinkled over the rock-surface. It's not Liathach; it's not even a Munro: it's just a small mountain of the furthest west. And the descent off the back is more quartzite: a wilderness of bare white rock, stones, green rock-pools and sudden low crags around the rock-pools.

And it goes on. After the first mile I'm feeling uneasy. This isn't hillwalking. I'm at home on hills, but this is an alien planet. I go over a pile of rocks and round a green sterile pool, and the sun sinks behind grey clouds towards a grey horizon. I'd like there to be another person, I'd like there to be an eagle or a sheep or anything. The grey sky and the grey ground understand each other perfectly, but neither of them has anything to do with a living hillwalker bravely kitted out in red breathable fabric.

I get more nervous, and start taking unnecessary compass bearings. And at last I climb over a pile of stones and find an

left: The low route heads up Coire Lair to the pass at its head. The high one crosses mountains on the left – including Sgorr Ruadh, above the walkers

ordinary peat-hag. Rough boggy grass and ordinary peat have never been so likeable, and never mind if the map's path going through the pass actually doesn't. For there's a cheerful stream, and a fellow living creature, even if that living creature is only a tussock of heather. And now, to reach the intended camp at Coire na Poite, there's nothing to do but another 4 miles (6km) of lovely living heather.

But I don't. A birch-wood, some flat grass and a tinkling waterfall make an irresistible composition, requiring only the addition of a simple orange triangle. I'm supposed to be testing this tent, so when I lie on my back for half an hour gazing at the midge-netting, this isn't the subsidence of emotional turmoil, this is the scientific study of insects.

The midge-netting appears to be OK.

DAY FIVE

There's just one barrier left between me and the sea. The wide flat-topped Corbett called Beinn Bhan looks like nothing much when seen between the Achnashellach spiky ones. It's when you get close you realise that though the top is flat, the front is not. The front is, in fact, four corries of vertical sandstone, and the ridges between aren't ridges but huge round rock-features called the Limpet and the Pot.

You may not think so from the spelling, but Gaelic is a curiously simple language, and direct. A'Chioch is a limpet, but it's also a breast. And while 600ft (200m) may be quite a size for a breast, it's even more of a size for a limpet. Actually, A'Poite, the pot, is upside-down to drain and has a nipple on the top, so they're really both breasts, and up between them, in whatever's Gaelic for cleavage, is the rock-backed campsite. I visit it anyway: it's well worth it.

There's a preliminary loch, with sandy beaches, placed so as to reflect A'Chioch and A'Poite. ('Hashish' and 'Opiate' suggests my bewildered spellchecker. Not bad, for a computer that's never been near the place.) Then there are great red boulders, short rock-steps with a path winding through or occasionally climbing up, and a rowan tree growing out sideways. As you get close, the side of the Poite hangs out over your head. And then your chin rises to the corrie floor. It's flat and grassy, and it has three lochans for the crags to dip their feet in. Great gullies drop scree into the back corners, and the Chioch and the Poite frame the outward view. What else is that view but the Achnashellach spiky ones, looking a little bit punkish and immature when seen from inside this massive place of crag.

So then I go down, and it's just as well I remembered the way down on the way up, as it's not at all obvious through the rock-steps. Round the bottom of the Poite, the next one's Coire na Fhamhair, the Giant's Corrie. (Obvious, really. Who else could use a 500ft-deep pot?) The Giant's Corrie contains a sandstone buttress that's 800ft (250m), but it just fits in neatly. I'm looking at the triangle of buttress that forms the corrie's north ridge. It looks impossible, then merely almost impossible, and then, suddenly, perfectly all right. Which is what the SMC's Corbetts book said it would be.

There is rock, but there is also grass. Walk sideways along the grass until the rock looks possible, and then go up the rock and find the next grass. It's not frightening, it's fine. What's not fine is the weather at the top. The cloud's down, and down thick, and the summit may be flat, but it's surrounded by very large drops.

Still, it isn't creepy like that quartzite. Mist and stonefields and a crag to walk over if you

go wrong is OK by me – this is something I know how to do. Going up is easy, of course, to find the trig point. Down is a compass-bearing, and the stopwatch for eight minutes, at which point the slope should steepen slightly. It does and so it's time for the next compass-bearing. It's irrational to be happy in such circumstances, but happy I am. And I find the tricky little col without falling over a single one of the crags.

Here a long valley winds into the sandstone. Dripping crags look better from below than from up on top where you couldn't see them even if it wasn't misty. I walk the long valley, past the black sprawling loch, and lo! the stalkers' path on the map actually exists. The valley bends, and there at the end is grey sea, and the grey cones of Glamaig and other hills of Skye, no longer horizon-spikes but close enough to sail to in a little boat.

The path widens and becomes a track with mountain-bikers. The track enters rhododendrons and becomes a road. Gorse bushes smell sweet in a still evening, and behind the gorse bushes is the sea. The Applecross Hotel does first-rate bar meals, but it's odd to shut out the spiky mountains and eat surrounded by human beings.

above: Britain's most crag-backed camp site, in Coire na Poite of Beinn Bhan

Beauly to Applecross: The Route

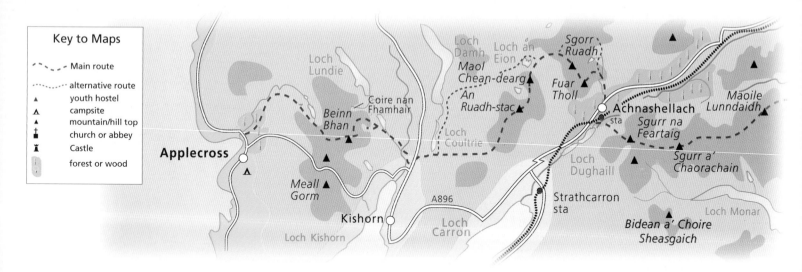

Key to Maps

- - - - Main route
.... alternative route
▲ youth hostel
🛆 campsite
▲ mountain/hill top
✝ church or abbey
⊠ Castle
🌲 forest or wood

BEAULY TO ACHNASHELLACH

■ Head straight inland from Beauly, taking a forest track to Loch nam Bonnach. Above Loch nan Eun, a track leads W above Gleann Goibhre. Leave it where it bends N (GR395479) for a tough, heathery ascent to Beinn a' Bha'ach Ard.

■ An easier ridge leads W over Carn nan Gearran Bana to the four Strathfarrar Munros: Sgurr na Ruaidhe, Carn nan Gobhar, Sgurr a' Choire Ghlais and Sgurr Fhuar-thuill.

■ After the final top, Sgurr na Fearstaig, a transverse ridge of heather and rock called Druim Dubh leads to An Sidhean. Drop steeply W into the valley of Coire Fionnarach – the stalkers' path on the map here is not traceable on the ground. Ascend immediately S of Loch a' Chlaidheimh onto Maoile Lunndaidh. Drop W over Carn nam Fiaclan to the two small lochans in the col north of Bidean an Eoin Deirg (GR106453). The key to the intimi-dating slope ahead is the spur immediately W of the upper part of the Abhainn Srath Mhuilich. Grassy hollows among schisty outcrops lead to the ridge of Sgurr a' Chaorachain.

■ After Sgurr Choinnich drop to the Bealach Bhearnais for a steep pull onto

Sgurr na Feartaig. Head W until an excellent stalkers' path leads down through Achnashellach Forest to Achnashellach. The footbridge over the River Carron does not exist, but the wide ford can usually be crossed. Otherwise, there is a bridge on the forest road 2½ miles (4km) upstream (GR047493).

ACHNASHELLACH TO APPLECROSS

■ After Achnashellach there is a choice of **high** and **low** routes to the A896 at Loch an Loin.

■ The **low route** follows a good path up Coire Lair to cross the Bealach Ban and the Bealach na Lice. After Loch an Eion, cross a rough valley head to join another path at GR904503. This leads down SW to the head of Loch Damh. Turn S to Loch an Loin.

■ Meanwhile, the **high route** forks left in Coire Lair to reach a lochan N of Fuar Tholl (GR971492). From here ascend SE, immediately to the left of the imposing Mainreachan Buttress. Go down Fuar Tholl's W ridge to climb Sgorr Ruadh.

■ Descend NW to rejoin the stalkers' path at Bealach Ban. Follow the path SW to the Bealach na Lice. The best way up Maol Chean-dearg is to contour left (S), to gain its E spur, and go up to left of its

crest. Cross An Ruadh-stac and quartzite wilderness beyond to join another path at the Bealach a' Ghlas-chnoic (GR900450). This leads down to Loch an Loin.

■ Once over the A896, cross moors N of Couldoran to join a path on the slopes of Beinn Bhan. A visit to the spectacular Coire na Poite is a must. A small path leads up through low sandstone crags into the corrie. Return, and contour into the next corrie to the N (Coire na Fhamhair). Its broad northern spur (GR813459) gives an easy scramble of low crags and grass ledges onto the plateau.

■ From Beinn Bhan's summit, head W to the Bealach nan Arr and drop N into Coire Attadale. After 2 miles (3km) pick up a path that leads out to the sea at Applecross Bay.

ESSENTIAL INFORMATION

Start: Beauly, Ross & Cromarty
Finish: Applecross village, Wester Ross
Distance: 80 miles (130km)
Distance on roads: 4 miles (6km)
Total ascent: 23,000ft (7000m), reduced by 5000ft

(1500m) if the **LOW ROUTE** is taken through the Achnashellach hills
Time: 5 days (of 16ml/26km, with 4500ft/1400m of ascent) for a strong party
Terrain: High ridges and steep mountains in seriously remote country. A technically easy (Grade 1) scramble onto Beinn Bhan

ACCESS

Stalking season is mid-August to mid-October. Start at Muir of Ord and join the Foul Weather
Alternative at Loch Orrin for a good low-level route on rights of way throughout

DISTANCE CHART (cumulative)

5	MLS	KM	COMMENTS
Beauly	0	0	
(Achnashellach omitting Craig)	(43)	(69)	
Craig	45	73	bunkhouse only
Achnashellach	48	77	hotel only
A 896	64	103	no facilities
Applecross	79	127	

NB: This distance chart is **not** incomplete. These are the only points on the crossing with facilities of any kind

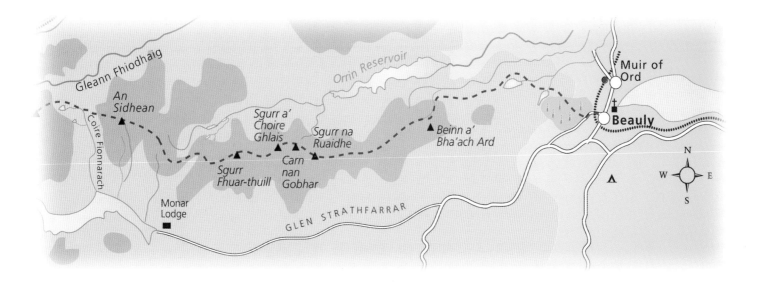

MAPS AND GUIDES

OS Landrangers Nos 26, 25, 24.

There is no guidebook to this crossing, and walkers undertaking it should be capable of finding and following their own route from the map

TRANSPORT

Beauly has a railway station, though it is often more convenient to take the train to Inverness and then a bus. Applecross has a daily post-bus (not Sundays) to Achnasheen on the Inverness-to-Skye railway. Three days into the route, Achnashellach is also on the Skye railway

FOUL WEATHER ALTERNATIVE

Orrin Reservoir, Gleann Fhiodhaig, Torridon, Diabeg (alternative foul weather finish)

TOURIST INFORMATION

North Kessock 01463 731505
Lochcarron 01520 722357
Ullapool 01854 612135

above: Crossing the moss on the second day of the long ridge. Sgurr Fhuar-thuill ahead

Solway to North Sea
North to the Forth

A nd so we arrive at the edge of the world, where the map has 'Here bee Dragons' picked out in Tourist Information blue hatching. Go for a long walk in the Scottish Lowlands and you've stepped off the last page of the guidebook into the Unknown. There are no stiles and waymarks along the pink dotted line on the map. In fact there's no pink dotted line. You don't walk measured miles towards a bunkhouse whose facilities are listed in your little book. You walk in hope, and the friendliness or otherwise of the natives is going to matter.

right: Just west of Sandyhills, on the Solway coast path that starts off the northward walk to the Forth

below: Dinghy but not dingy: the neat, white-painted cottages of Kippford at the start of North to the Forth. A few bedraggled palm trees indicate that we are still in the tropical South. Edinburgh will be chillier

GALLOWAY GRANITE: DALBEATTIE TO DUMFRIES

Dalbeattie's a chilly grey town of granite blocks, but in less than five minutes I was under brown autumn beeches. Little crags stuck up into the wood, and there was a loch to walk round while the sun shone in sideways at trunk level. Even when it became an ordinary forest road, it was a road with a view – small arms of the sea crept into the golden landscape, and reassured me that I'd get to the coast, and my Barnbarroch bed, by bedtime.

Along the Solway we walk for 6 miles (10km) over lichened rocks and sharp inlets. Among the jellyfish and old shoes float splinters from long-shattered smuggler ships. Below, the wide mud is decorated in abstract patterns by the long nets of the salmon fishers. On a crisp, cold day the mountains of England rise out of the sea with snow along their tops.

One of the peculiarities of this walk is that it crosses to the east coast by travelling almost directly north. Another of its peculiarities is that in order to do so, it sets off almost directly south. What does make sense is to take an initial half-day of 10 miles (15km) and spend the first night at the B&B of Port o' Warren. As well as an all-night sea view, this gives reasonable onward stages by Dumfries and Burleywhag. A gentler schedule would be to stop at New Abbey, Dalswinton and Kettleton Byre to Elvanfoot before the challenge of the Culters. Why, we're almost at Edinburgh already ….

Back in the Dark Ages, no journey was complete without an ugly green monster sprawling across the path. Today we have to make do with the Forest of Boreland. Torn limb from limb with sharp claws you will be, but only slightly. There's a quarter mile – a mere 400m – of brushwood and bramble, with wet ditches below and gay yellow gorse closing in overhead. The quarter mile is necessary: it's the

link through Forest Enterprise land between the shining mud of Solway and a useful small hill called Criffel.

Criffel is a hump of speckled grey granite, with the same mud-and-England views seen from higher up. More intimate views of mud are on the descent path. And already, as I drop into New Abbey, it's time for another sunset. At the tall pink arches of Sweetheart Abbey, the journey northward becomes one through the history of Scotland. Under the grass of the abbey is buried John Baliol – known as Toom Tabard.

Toom Tabard is a mocking nickname meaning 'Empty Jacket'. John Baliol was King of Scotland, appointed to that post by King Edward of England. He was a very temporary king, who soon rebelled against Edward, was defeated in battle, and retired to his estate in France. His widow, the Lady Devorgilla, built Sweetheart Abbey in his memory, and also founded Baliol College. The fact that Baliol College is at Oxford rather than St Andrews shows how little the difference between England and Scotland mattered to civilised and intelligent people of the late thirteenth century.

A long walk in the lowlands is patched together out of town woods, dog-walking paths and fishermen's paths, forest roads and empty hilltops. The scratches are part of the package.

What wasn't part of the package was trying to do the easy bit through Mabie Forest in the dark. Well, not actual darkness, as a big white moon danced among the treetops. Somewhere behind the branches there was a silvery lake. The forest road was wide and pale, and even under the trees I could step out confidently on the soft needles. The flash of the torch picked out a waymark pole; a deer paused in the moonlight and wondered what that noisy thing was at the other end of the clearing. And then the White Trail ended suddenly in an ocean of clear-fell.

The thing to do is to take it very slowly, and enjoy the pattern of silvery twigs against the black water of a rut-puddle, and not mind too much that the only way round the silvery twigs is to walk through that black water. I got out to a forest road, but it was the wrong one. The right road was just down the slope, so I stepped carefully off the edge, slid, tripped, and ended upside down in a bramble patch. The most interesting bit of all was lying in the brambles and realising that a further somersault would be required to get the feet downslope from the head ....

Next day at dawn I escaped from Mabie Forest and found the field path to the River Nith. The estuary's salty banks lead straight into the centre of Dumfries.

GREEN LOWTHERS: DUMFRIES TO ELVANFOOT

By the time we reach Dumfries, Scottish history has advanced some twenty important years. A Franco-Scottish baron, Robert de Brus, has quarrelled with Toom Tabard's brother-in-law and slain him with a dagger before the altar of Greyfriars Kirk. Greyfriars Kirk is no more; the spot was marked by a small plaque above the freezer cabinet in Wm Low's – but is now Blockbuster Video (and yes, they have several copies of *Braveheart*). The murder didn't matter but the sacrilege did. Bruce had helped England's Edward defeat John Baliol, but now he was out of the game of 'swear fealty to both sides and grab another Scottish Estate'. His only way forward was to oppose everyone and go for the big one. Guerrilla skirmishes in the Galloway hills led to victory at Bannockburn, and the start of Scotland's four centuries of independence.

Meanwhile, the Lady Devorgilla has been commemorating Baliol again. The Devorgilla Bridge across the Nith originally had thirteen arches and was the longest in Europe. It was thus the fourteenth-century equivalent of the Forth Road Bridge. Such massive engineering projects are not necessarily the sign of civilisation. Still, while England was beating itself up in the Wars of the

left: The walk through Scotland starts at the Solway, but the walk through Scottish history starts here at Sweetheart Abbey. The last king of Scotland ever to swear fealty to England is buried beneath the ruins

below: Devorgilla Bridge, at Dumfries. The walk passes out of Galloway over this fourteenth-century equivalent of the Forth Road Bridge

Roses, Scotland had direct links with Europe, and was equal partner with France and the Low Countries in literature, music and scholarship.

I passed the morning meandering up the River Nith with cool sunlight sparkling on the damp black rubberwear of the fishermen. Then a stony track led up into the Forest of Ae. Ae is Britain's shortest place-name, and the trudge through the trees was over in a couple of hours. At Mitchellslacks I stepped onto the network of paths, tracks and old roads through the Lowther Hills.

The Lowthers are rounded sheepfarming hills. On Gana Hill you stand on yellow grasses and gaze at a grey reservoir and miles and miles more of yellow grasses. The surprise is that the tracks through the hills are very much better than the hills themselves. Streams have carved steep valleys with waterfalls and wild goats. The Capel Valley in, and Glenaggart out, are remote and enclosed, with heather sides and a green track along the bottom.

In terms of things, Durisdeer offers little more than a cold water tap and a simple red phone box. With ideas, though, Durisdeer is well equipped. At the half-way point of the walk, scenery intersects history, and literature meets the funerary arts. The Romans came down through the Well Pass, and the characters in Salman Rushdie's *Satanic Verses* drove up the A702 and wandered over the tops around the village. There's a Covenanting martyr in the graveyard, but the more interesting burial is round the back.

In an annex on the north side of the church is the tomb of the 2nd Earl of Queensberry. He has it all. There are marble draperies and barley-sugar marble columns. There is a long Latin inscription. There are four marble cherubs weeping marble tears.

It must have cost a bomb; and oddly enough, we know how it was paid for. Scotland's four centuries as a separate nation started in Dumfries with a stabbing, and ended in 1707 when Queensberry signed up the Treaty of Union with England and closed down the Scottish Parliament. For this service he received a pension of £3,000.

At nine on an autumn morning, not much goes on in Nithsdale. I met a dog-walker; two hours later I met a shepherd. Frost was on the fields, and in the clear air Criffel looked a lot less than two days away behind me.

The Enterkin Pass takes a route of great beauty through the northern Lowthers, first on a green shelf above the wooded stream, then through a slot in the hills to a pass at 1800ft (550m). This beauty was little appreciated by the SSEB, who have strung a low-voltage power line all the way through. It was appreciated even less by Bonnie Prince Charlie. Having marched as far as Derby before realising that England was not going to rise on his behalf and throw out German George, he came through the Enterkin in the last dark days of 1745, with his army demoralised but not defeated behind him. Defeat would come later, on the grim winter moor of Culloden.

Sixty years earlier, a dramatic rescue took place in the valley. Covenantors ambushed a redcoat patrol and freed two prisoners. The small gorge is 'Keltie's Linn', named after the soldier shot dead in the incident. Covenantors were Presbyterian Protestants who claimed the right to run their own churches rather than have bishops inflicted on them by the King. During the

left: Durisdeer, below the Lowther Hills. The village is short in facilities but long in history

'Killing Times' of the late 1600s they received savage persecution, to which they responded sometimes with meekness and sometimes with assassination. For the rest of the walk we shall follow the hundreds of Covenantors who were not rescued but led away to Edinburgh to trial and execution in Greyfriars Kirkyard.

At the pass top comes a sudden change. Green gives way to brown heather, burnt black in patches to promote fresh growth for grouse. Ahead lies a day and a half of bleak Border Country. At our feet is an abandoned industrial landscape. We can discuss endlessly whether Durisdeer, behind us, is the prettiest village in Scotland; but Wanlockhead ahead is certainly the highest, at 1680ft (560m). Around it lie the interesting remains of seventeenth-century lead mines.

During the summer months you can put on a hard hat and take a trip into the hill. The beam engine was an engineering marvel of its age: a pump to raise water from the deep shafts, itself powered by the falling water of a nearby stream. On the way out you'll pass the remains of a later pump that was the first piece of steam-powered machinery ever.

After Leadhills, the walk takes the easy way out of the Lowthers, down an abandoned railway. The Culter Fells ahead will provide sufficient difficulty.

YELLOW GRASS COUNTRY: ELVANFOOT TO BLYTH BRIDGE

It's odd that these borderlands, once the most fought-over, are now the most peaceful bits of Britain. This applies to the Welsh Marches of Offa's Dyke Path. It also applies here in the Culters. Where once English and Scots marauded back and forth driving each other's stolen cattle, now wander only a few sheep. The shepherd's quad bike has done much to make this country pleasantly walkable: its faint pathway among the tussocks means you can stroll, relax and enjoy the view.

That view is widening. Culter Fell is the highest point of the walk. Here you start to feel the shape of Scotland. Behind are the gentle valleys of the Southern Uplands. Ahead is a wide plain, busy with industry. Beyond it, above the haze, small white blobs and spikes are Ben More and Ben Lomond under early snow.

There's even a dusting of snow up on Culter Fell, and the friendly footprints of last week's hillwalker. November sunset starts at half-past three, and you can stop for a bar meal as early as five without missing any of the evening daylight.

Cool autumn air means you aren't desperate for a bath or shower – certainly not needing one enough to pass the remaining four hours to bedtime in hot water. So you just have to pull on an extra fleece and keep

left: The track along the Grains Burn enters the remote and rounded Culter Fells

going. I fumbled across the Broughton Heights by moonlight and torchlight. And streetlight – for the Broughtons project into the wide Midlothian plain. The landscape is picked out in lines of sodium orange, with a moving bracelet of ice-white from the evening commuters on the A702, and the pale sparks of a train gradually crossing the scene. Jagged Pentlands stand against the sunset like the teeth of a bloodstained saw. Night walking is necessarily slower and more thoughtful. Eyes widen to take in the faint streak of a path. Mind widens to take in surreal luminous landscape. Everything goes very quiet.

PENTLANDS AND EDINBURGH:
BLYTH BRIDGE TO LEITH

The path below the Pentlands has been used since Roman times. We can imagine the Lady Devorgilla, riding side-saddle on her sturdy Galloway pony, heading up to Edinburgh to hire some Flemish stone-masons. Splashing through the West Water, she trades Solway scandal with her retainers – but at the same time she's looking forward to some theological chit-chat with the city intellectuals. Maybe a university like Oxford for Edinburgh – why not?

Mary, bewildered girl-queen, came this way on pilgrimage to the White House of St Ninian in distant Whithorn. Noblemen escort her, showing all deference while working out how to stop her being so sinfully tolerant of Protestants.

In 1666 there pass along the road a few score of Galloway country folk. Barefoot, armed with sticks and not particularly dangerous-looking

above: Looking back along the Pentland ridge to Scald Law and the Kips

right: Heart of Midlothian: the view back from the Pentlands to the Broughton Heights. Smoke from burning heather hangs across the Midlothian plain

above: Edinburgh Castle. Although North to the Forth keeps its walkers off the streets for most of the way through the city, it makes an exception for the Royal Mile. The famous thoroughfare runs down from Castle Hill to Holyrood Palace at the base of Arthur's Seat

muskets – a rabble, you'd say, until they pause for prayer before crossing the ford. Persecuted at home, these Covenantors are carrying the war to the enemy in the grandly-titled 'Pentland Rising'. Already, men with rather better muskets are coming out of Edinburgh to meet them.

And here's Queensberry, heading up from his Nithsdale estate in 1707. This close to the capital the road has a better surface, and he can relax from grabbing the hand-straps of his carriage and spend the last few hours of the journey preparing his mind. The allies are in position, the opponents have been paid off, but no committee ever wants to shut up or shut down, and parliaments in particular are noisy beasts. The carriage sways gently but does not disturb his concentration as it crosses the newly built bridge of the West Water.

Does Dumfries to Edinburgh seem like a longish trip? Six times a year a stonemason's son called Thomas Carlyle passed along the road, pleased and proud to walk a hundred miles to study mathematics. Perhaps by West Linton he's in a crowd of young men, joking in mock-Latin, cursing the high-speed carriages that spatter them with mud, leaping up to dangle from low branches, as they head for a new term at Edinburgh's ancient University.

November walking can be chilly and grim. There's a lot of mist and rain, and not very many buses. Trees are leafless, grass is brown and paths are mud. Worst of all is the way the day switches straight from mid-morning to late afternoon without any useful walking hours between.

Slight compensation is the odd November day when the clouds roll back and November's watery sun emerges from behind a cold front. They're burning the moors and smoke drifts across the Midlothian plain, with the hills of Midlothian sticking their noses up into the clear air above.

The path may be mud but it's frozen hard, and Pentland grasses take on surreal shades of orange and mauve into the blue distance. And then you're passing through a blood-red sunset. Edinburgh lies below as a sea of bright orange, with the black shapes of its seven hills outlined against the glow.

Maybe such a day doesn't really compensate for the grey weeks around it, the map-reading with frozen fingers in the mist, the boots soggy and swollen to double their size. But you can't spend all winter by the fireside reading long-distance walking books.

An Edinburgh inhabitant on Allermuir tells of a clever way under the ring road – 'a path for strollers', it sounds just the thing. And it is: a strip of hedgehog and bramble between the house-backs. The Water of Leith winds its way in below street-level, dark beneath its trees. It splashes in the darkness, and sends up a rich aroma of decomposing autumn litter. After a disturbing moment under neon lamps, earth steps lead up from a shopping street onto the towpath of the Union Canal. Ice on the canal makes crackling patterns around the floating beer-cans.

I've been walking in the night for two hours, but along the Royal Mile it's still only early evening. Tourists are examining pub menus, buying newspapers and climbing in and out of buses. Ahead of me, in Holyrood Palace, Prince Charlie was dancing the eightsome reel when he should have been out chasing the defeated English. On the right, in St Giles' Cathedral, Jenny Geddes flung her stool at the Bishop of St Andrews and started the Reformation. And down at the bottom they're still busy building us our new Parliament.

Undoubtedly Arthur's Seat must (all respect to Cave Hill, Belfast) be Britain's finest urban mountain. One of the early Scottish mountaineers brought his Alpine guide over to Scotland, and as an exercise in perspective asked him how long to climb Arthur's Seat? The guide studied the crags and precipices. 'A strong party,' he judged, 'should get up in less than three hours.'

I ascended in twenty minutes by way of the Gutted Haddie but still couldn't forget that here, in the darkness of the seventeenth century, Robert Wringhim encountered the Devil sitting on a stone. (This was in James Hogg's *Confessions of a Justified Sinner*. Satan explained that God knows everything, including whether you yourself are headed for Heaven or Hell. And since this matter is already decided, you might as well stop worrying and have a hell of a time while still alive.)

A green hump on Leith Links is where English guns stood in 1560. Mary of Guise, who was French but Queen of Scotland, was besieged in Leith by the combined forces of Protestant Scots and England's Elizabeth. Actually, Mary of Guise was the Queen Mother; Mary Stewart was Queen of Scots and married to the Dauphin of France. The politics of the time were complicated, and not good for Scotland. Even today, the fine new building of the Scottish Executive peers nervously inwards between the house-backs of Leith, but in the other direction gazes out across the harbour towards Europe.

For the defeated Covenantors, Leith was just the continuation of their journey to the slave-huts of the West Indies or shipwreck on the rocks of Orkney. But for us now it is only the brief bus-ride back into the city. We can finish up the sandwiches on Calton Hill and annoy the shoppers with our rucksacks along busy Princes Street. We can linger in Edinburgh, enjoying its art galleries and outdoor shops. Or we can appreciate the way the noisome swamp that once protected the castle has been turned into a useful railway station, and whisk ourselves away to whatever lesser city we come from.

overleaf: Edinburgh at night, from Allermuir. Arthur's Seat stands above the sea of streetlights at back right

North to the Forth: The Route

DALBEATTIE TO NEW ABBEY

■ From Dalbeattie town centre, Union Street leads E into woods (Town Wood). Marked trails (blue then yellow) lead to E of a small loch. From GR844600 forest tracks lead SE then S to Barnbarroch.

■ Take the road to Kippford Post Office, where the Jubilee Path forks left to Rockcliffe. Where the road turns uphill out of Rockcliffe, the signposted coast path sets off to Sandyhills.

■ Follow minor roads N to Drumstinchall farm, where a track cuts a corner NE. Turn right on the B793 to the Old Schoolhouse (GR921585), where a path leads across to Dunmuck. Turn right for 400yd/m, when a path leads up into the forest on the left. This soon turns right to meet a forest road. Turn left up this. The second side-track on the right short-cuts over the hill, to rejoin the forest road at its endpoint where there is a shed (GR933579).

■ Head NE through nasty brushwood and scrub for 400yd/m to a forest track. Tracks lead up through the wood to end above Redbank Hill at the Parruten Burn (GR938597). Follow the stream up, then turn left along the top edge of the trees. A small path to the left of a wall leads to a wall gap near the summit of Boreland Hill. Cross a rough col to climb Criffel.

■ A muddy path leads down over Knockendoch to Mid Glen. Just before the stream, a field gate on the right starts an unmarked right-of-way path. Follow a plantation edge to a track leading NE into the edge of New Abbey. Turn left along the A710 for 50yd/m, then right (to the left of the school). A path crosses playing fields then turns left to Sweetheart Abbey.

NEW ABBEY TO DUMFRIES

■ Leave New Abbey on the Beeswing road for ¾ mile (1km), then turn right on a forest track ('Private Road'). After 1½ miles (2km) a path turns off left, to become a forest track running NW. Cross a minor road (GR933692) and take tracks past Lochaber Loch into Mabie Forest.

■ A forest road, or the Brown Trail on the right, leads to Mabie House. Those without the Mabie trail map should now head N past Burnside. Those with the Mabie map follow tracks or trails to GR943723. Slant down E, with a wiggle to left half way down, to find an old track running SE out of the forest. It reaches a minor road at GR953718. Directly opposite is the signed path into Islesteps.

■ The right-of-way by Cargen Pow is currently impassable, so follow the A710 to Laghall to gain the Nithside path into Dumfries.

DUMFRIES TO ELVANFOOT

■ Cross the stone footbridge (Devorgilla Bridge) and take the Burns Walk alongside the Nith (E bank) to Dalscone. Turn left just before a small sewage works to rejoin the Nith. From Carnshalloch, a waymarked path follows the flood bank NW, rejoining the river. In a plantation turn right to Bellholm farm and follow roads past Duncow to a track end below Braehead (GR948843). Take this track uphill (N), to pass left of Shaws farm. 100yd/m before Pennyland turn right on an inconspicuous old track NW into the Forest of Ae.

■ Forest roads lead N to Loch Ettrick. Turn right along the road for 2 miles (3km) to Mitchellslacks, where a track runs up the Capel Burn to Burleywhag bothy.

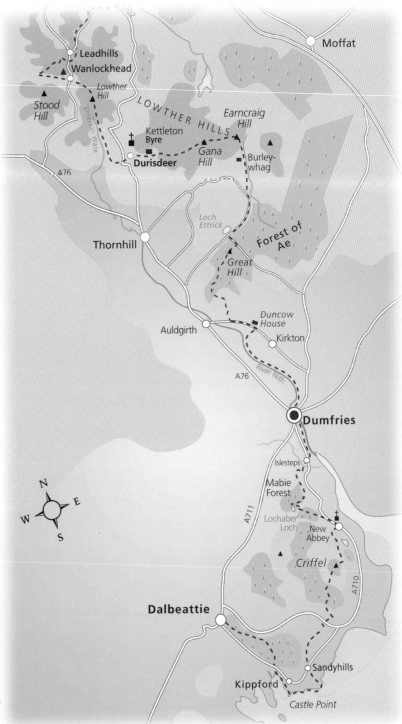

above: The track below Garroch Fell

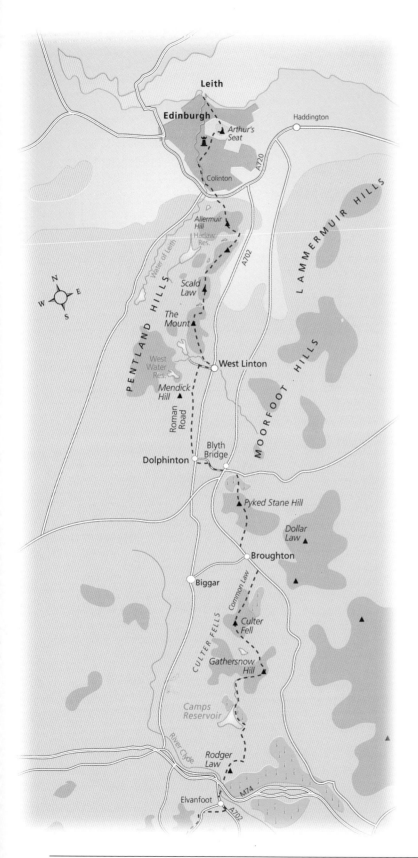

■ Ascend the rocky S spur of Earncraig Hill, and follow fences over Gana Hill. Descend the heathery W end of Garroch Fell (quad bike track on the SW flank is easier) to a track. This leads NW past Kettleton Byre bothy to Durisdeer.

■ Small roads and a brief field track lead W to Muiryhill then N to near Inglestone. A green path runs N to join the Enterkin Burn and climb to the Enterkin Pass (GR883106). It joins the Lowther access road for 400yd/m, then turns down left at a Southern Upland Way waymark into Wanlockhead.

■ Follow the Southern Upland Way through the old mining area for 800yd/m, then cross the valley to a side-valley running NE. An old path crosses above the head of the Snar Water to a gate, where a track descends to the B797. Cross to Leadhills Station. The former railbed runs down the Shortcleuch Valley to Elvanfoot.

ELVANFOOT TO BROUGHTON

■ Pass under the main railway to a footbridge over the River Clyde. Once under the M74, take forest roads up NE to the masts on Lady Cairn. From Rodger Law a spur drops NE to the West Water. Keep round to right of enclosed ground around Harecleuch, then cross the valley floor to a sheep dipper (GR010193). Cross Yearngill Head to Camps Reservoir.

■ Tracks run past the reservoir and up Grains Burn. Follow Hillshaw Burn onto the ridge, then E around the flank of Hillshaw Head to reach a fence on the ridgeline. Fences are followed over Gathersnow Hill, Culter Fell and Cardon Hill to Common Law.

■ From Knowe Knitting descend NE until the slope eases, then turn down E, to cross a boggy stream and go up the tree-gap opposite to a forest road. Follow it NE to its end, then keep ahead along a broad ride. After 300yd/m this turns left, downhill, for 200yd/m. Now turn right along a wide tree-gap to the forest edge.

■ Follow a wall to the right for a few yards, then up Whitslade Hill and on to the 'Fort and Settlement' above Broughton. Follow spur N to a gate at the top of a narrow plantation (GR111357), and go down to left of this to the minor road leading into Broughton.

Key to Maps

– – – – – Main route

········· alternative route

▲ youth hostel

△ campsite

▲ mountain/hill top

♰ church or abbey

♙ Castle

▮ forest or wood

BROUGHTON TO WEST LINTON

■ A track passes Broughton Place into the valley of Hollows Burn. At the valley head, a faint track runs up to the col Clover Law/Broomy Side GR124393. Follow fence over Green Law to the trig on Pyked Stane Hill (just 'Broughton Heights' on Landranger) and to Wether Law.

■ As the ground steepens off Wether Law, head down just E of N into a wide tree-gap with a stream. After 100yd/m a forest road starts up left. This leads down N until a farm track runs out of the trees to reach the A72. Head NW on the verge of this fairly busy road for ¾mile (1km) to the junction with the A701.

■ Cross onto a minor road, and at Newmill turn off left onto a track to Dolphinton. Turn right, then take the minor road 'Garvald' for 200yd/m, then the signposted track below Mendick Hill to West Linton.

WEST LINTON TO COLINTON

■ From the phone box on the A702, a riverside path leads up through steep woods to right (E) of the Lyne Water. Tracks lead through Stonypath. Turn off up open slopes to Mount Maw and The Mount.

■ Grassy slopes lead down E to the dam of the North Esk Reservoir. Cross Spittal Hill and Green Law to the col at the head of Eight Mile Burn. Clear paths run along the main Pentland Ridge, crossing the rocky top of West Kip, then East Kip, Scald Law and Carnethy to Turnhouse Hill. Turn down E, to a footbridge (GR228631) near Flotterstone Inn.

■ Turn right on track, then left on tarred track up-valley. After 300yd/m a path on the right is signed 'Castlelaw'. Follow waymarks round to right of Castlelaw farm.
A pink-gravelled military road runs up N to the base of Allermuir Hill. Path beside fence goes straight up to the trig and viewpoint indicator. It's quite a view – all of Edinburgh.

■ Rejoin the military road down off the hill to a building by the Howden Burn (GR222672).

DISTANCE CHART (cumulative)

	MLS	KM	COMMENTS		MLS	KM	COMMENTS
Dalbeattie	0	0		Wanlockhead	72	116	YH
Kippford	5	8		Leadhills	74	119	
Rockcliffe	6	10	hotel, cafe	Elvanfoot	80	129	B&B only
Sandyhills	11	18		Broughton	100	161	
New Abbey	25	40		Blyth Bridge	106	171	inn only
Mabie Forest	30	48	hotel only	Dolphinton	108	174	B&B only
Dumfries	35	56		West Linton	112	180	
Kirkton	41	66		Flotterstone	123	198	inn only
Dalswinton (+ 1 ml)	44	71		Colinton	127	204	
Burleywhag	57	92	bothy	Arthur's Seat	133	214	
Kettleton Byre	63	101	bothy	Leith	136	219	
Durisdeer	65	105	no facilities				

■ Head N to a track running N into woods. At a track below turn left, 'Bonaly'. After 400yd/m is another signpost. Here bear right 'Laverockdale' to a streamside path under the ring road at GR217680. It heads NE for 400yd/m. Turn left on track that becomes 'Dreghorn Loan' into Colinton.

COLINTON TO LEITH

■ Cross the B701 to steps descending 'Colinton Parish Church'. Pass to left of the church, to a delightful path alongside (to left of) Water of Leith. After 300yd/m it climbs left to an old railway.

■ After 800yd/m steps lead down to a lane below, and this runs down to cross the Water of Leith. Now the right bank is followed to the busy Lanark Road (A70).

■ Turn right under the massive concrete bridge of the Union Canal. Steps on the left lead up onto the towpath. This is followed to the canal's end at a roundabout on the Fountainbridge Road.

■ Turn right (E) to the Grassmarket. Steps on the left lead up to the castle esplanade. The Royal Mile runs down to the Palace of Holyroodhouse. Turn right into Holyrood Park.

■ The most interesting way up Arthur's Seat is to follow the cliff edge of Salisbury Crag to its end. Now the direct uphill by the Hawse is an eroded horror, but slant up right to the foot of crag, and slant up left along its base. Continuing the leftward slant gives a

path on bare rock to the very base of the rocky summit knoll.

■ Leave Arthur's Seat N past St Margaret's Loch, and pass under railway on Royal Park Place (GR276742). Head round to left of Meadowbank Sports Centre into Lochend Park. Just N of the park, a railway path passes sports fields to the Easter Road at GR271755.

■ Cross Leith Links and turn left into Queen Charlotte Street. Cross Leith Walk to Lamb's House (GR271765, marked 'NTS' on Landranger). Follow the quayside downstream to the last bridge over the Water of Leith and the outlook over Leith Docks.

ESSENTIAL INFORMATION

Start: Dalbeattie, Dumfries & Galloway
Finish: Leith Docks, Edinburgh
Distance: 140 miles (225km)
Distance on roads: 19 miles (31km)
Total ascent: 21,000ft (6400m)
Time: 8 days (of 17mls/28km), including a tough one over the Culter Fells of 20mls/32km with 4300ft/1300m of ascent. Between Dumfries and Wanlockhead, the Lowther bothies are the only on-route accommodation
Terrain: Paths and tracks, with very occasional off-path prickly bits, and grassy hilltops over the Culter Fells

MAPS

OS Landrangers Nos 84, 78, 72 and 66. Also useful are *Forests of Solway* from Forest Enterprise, Ae, Dumfriesshire (about £1) and a street

map of Edinburgh such as *Harveys Edinburgh Seven Hills*.
No guidebook, but *Lowther Hills* by Ronald Turnbull, *Lammermuirs* by Alan Hall (both published by Cicerone) help in places

ACCESS

Most of the walk is on established paths, open moor and hill, and forest plantations; but only a few miles are on rights-of-way. Although courteous and considerate walkers are unlikely to have difficulties, they should be aware that there is no legal entitlement to walk this route. Grouse shooting in S Lowthers and Broughton Heights 12 Aug–12 Dec

TRANSPORT

Dalbeattie is served by frequent buses from Dumfries (station and long-distance coach services). Edinburgh has excellent rail and coach links. Sandyhills, Rockcliffe, New Abbey and Dalswinton have buses to Dumfries. Elvanfoot and West Linton have buses to Dumfries and Edinburgh; Broughton has buses to Biggar 0345 090510

TOURIST INFORMATION

Dumfries 01387 253862
Abington 01864 502436
Peebles 01721 720138
Edinburgh 0131 473 3800

right: English Lake District from the Solway coast path. St Bees Head, endpoint of Wainwright's Coast-to-Coast, is just 22 miles (35km) away

The Rest of the Coast-to-Coasts

Northern Ireland

The Mountains of Mourne sweep down to the sea, as everybody knows; but they do so with such steepness that the high point of Northern Ireland, Slieve Donard, stands just 2.2 miles (3.5km) from the beach at Bloody Bridge.

The Mournes are granite mountains. Towers of granite totter along the ridgelines, and granite sand makes one truly splendid path, the Brandy Pad. It's a smugglers' way, that sneaks along the 2000ft (600m) contour, below the crags, above long views out into the Irish Sea. I unrolled my sleeping bag on Eagle Mountain and watched the night mist rise around the pointed cones of Slieve Bearnagh, the yellow sea-gleam of evening, the green-hedged lowlands fading into the grey.

Ireland's green really is greener, especially when the sun slants golden from the west, and the Mournes gradually go blue as I walk away. Ireland has no right-of-way network – the small farmers are Catholic and footpath officers are just another aspect of the Ancient Enemy. But Irish roads dance in and out among small rocky hills. There are few cars. Few, but friendly – everybody waves and one even drifted along beside me, wearing out his clutch for the sake of five minutes' conversation.

It was a little unsettling, though, that the friendly conversation consisted of warnings not to camp in the Belfast Hills. And then the little roads started to take me through the little towns. At Dromara I saw my first fortified police station. In Hillsborough they were preparing for the marching season, with bunting and a picture of the Queen 50 years ago, a poor likeness even then. But there are just too many Union Jacks, once you've realised that the Union Jack is there to intimidate. And up beside the Queen there's a redcoat cavalryman of about 1850. The redcoat is decorative, but back in 1850 his job was to kill Catholics.

The Lagan towpath led me into the city, where lamp-posts still carried (from an election that was weeks previously) pictures of Paisley. And then the signs changed, and I'd passed into Catholic West Belfast.

In 1969, gangs of Protestants stormed across this line, looting and setting fire to houses. Reading the history makes it easier to understand just why road signs here have been shot up with semi-automatic weapons; why pavements are covered in broken

right: Alongside the Mourne Wall on the ridge of Slievenaglogh. Northern Ireland has great walking, but as yet no great long-distance walk

glass; why walls carry the depressing slogan 'not a bullet, not an ounce'. But when I came onto what should have been, under the broken glass, a pleasant streamside path, and found it blocked with a burnt-out car, I'd had enough. I went back into Belfast and got on a boat.

Two miles ahead I'd have hit the Ulster Way, and that would have taken me all the way to Antrim's nine glens: 'you'll love it in the Glens. It's quite safe up there'. The Moyle Way runs on over hills of bog topped with basalt, and a fine coastal path leads to the famous Bushmills distillery. Hope is a virtue, particularly in the north of Ireland. There's going to be a great long-distance walk.

Southern Ireland

Various long-distance paths appear on the maps, but close examination shows them all to have a high content of road. Still, it's the place for those who want to walk into the unknown but not so unknown you have to learn Norwegian, Spanish or Japanese ....

Scotland

Beauly to Applecross is just one of many routes north of Inverness. Sea inlets in the east mean you can start well across and close to the mountains. In the west, though, you should keep on going as far as possible. The shortest such crossing, from Bonar Bridge by Gleann Beag to Loch Broom, is just 31 miles (50km) of spectacular country; sadly, though, the eastern half is on tarmac track.

Similarly, Highland and Grampian is just a sample of the crossings of the main mountain area. Any coast-to-coast here will be exciting and interesting, the one you devise for yourself the most interesting of all because you don't know how it's going to turn out. Highland Horseback (01466 700304) offers an equine version for those competent on four legs.

Small but shapely are the hills of the Scottish Lowlands – Lomonds and Ochils, Campsie Fells and Kilpatricks. No written route will ever gain approval from the multitude of landowners and countryside agencies. Nevertheless, the adaptable and courteous walker can make a most enjoyable crossing here (80ml/130km). Streetlight spilling out of the Forth/Clyde valley means you can march on night and day if you want ....

The Southern Upland Way (210ml/340km) looks good on the small-scale map, but has too much road and too many Christmas trees. Start, though, at Holy Island along St Cuthbert's Way; take to the hilltops over the central section; and finish over Cairnsmore of Fleet. By altering both ends and the middle you can get a Southern Upland Way that really is upland.

left: Bivvy bag dusk on Sgurr nan Coireachan – a high-level variant off Highland and Grampian

England

Northern England, with its path network and small hills of various sorts, offers many more than the two routes in this book. Start in the Wolds, the North York Moors or the Durham Dales: cross the Pennines at some point: end in Lakeland, Arnside or Bowland. Here too is the SUSTRANS coast-to-coast for cycles (150ml/250km). It runs from Whitehaven to Tynemouth, with alternatives of increasing severity for the more rugged sort of bike. It's good taken gently on a tourer, and just as good over Cross Fell on an all-terrain or mountain bike.

Crossings of Central England are rather too long, and rather too flat in the east. Across the south, though, are low chalk hills arranged usefully east–west. The Ridgeway path now runs from Lowestoft to Lyme Regis (350mls/550km). Another downland route, 'Channel to Channel', runs from Kent to the Mendips (240mls/400km). You could stride out fast over these pebbly tracks, except that there are just so many pubs along the way .... Most of the bad bits have been eliminated from the Thames path and it is becoming very popular. Footpaths through the Cotswolds lead on easily to the Bristol Channel (220mls/350km).

Across the SW Peninsula, the Two Moors Way (100mls/160km) is where I was going to go if the Uphill to Old Harry route hadn't worked so well.

Wales

The Cambrian Way (260mls/420km) was developed at the same time as our Snowdonia to Gower. It takes in even more mountains and has no low-level alternatives, and is the toughest recognised route outside Scotland.

If you're prepared to accept the English border as the 'coast' of Wales, there are crossings east to west that are short, varied and interesting. One starts at Clun, heads west over the Clun and Kerry Hills, continues over Pumlumon Fawr (Plynlimon) to Aberystwyth.

Why not combine Offa's Dyke from Prestatyn to Chirk Bank with the high ridges of the Berwyns, Arans and Cadair Idris, finishing at Barmouth?

In south Wales there's a fine route from Chepstow on the Severn Estuary to Fishguard, taking in the Black Mountains, Brecon Beacons and Mynydd Du before crossing the pretty hills of Carmarthenshire and Preseli. If you want to see a bit more of the Pembrokeshire Coast, you could extend the route to St Davids.

left: Wainwright's Coast-to-Coast leaves Lakeland at Ennerdale Water

overleaf: Last sight of the sea until the other side: looking back down Wasdale

The one you make up yourself

Uphill to Old Harry was one I made earlier. You can lift that south-west walk straight off the shelf, plug it in and set it going. However, that chapter is also intended as a manual on how to make your own way from Somewhere Interesting to Wherever You Fancy. Been planning a visit to your granny in Lancashire? Arrive on foot by way of the Forest of Bowland. The orange tide of Explorers at 1:25 000 is creeping up the country, and expected to reach the Scottish border in 2002 or so. In England anyway, a good map isn't hard to find.

The secret of easy DIY is to use ready-made components. These are not just the National Trails, but the prefabricated paths long and short on the Ordnance Survey's free Mapping Index, or in the Long Distance Walkers' Handbook. Some, like the West Mendip Way, are well-maintained and waymarked; without even looking at the map, you can follow them for miles and miles before you get lost. Even the Monarch's Way is an assurance that the necessary stile is there somewhere under the nettles.

Most home-made paths involve 'field studies' – invisible footpaths through nettle-beds and around field edges. Within the National Parks, the rights-of-way are almost all usable, with signposts where they meet public roads and waymarks where they meet each other. All necessary stiles and footbridges will exist. Outside the parks, in rural Somerset, wild Wales or muddy Sussex, it gets more interesting. Following untrodden footpaths through fields and hedges is navigation as tricky as any misted hill, though the penalty for getting it wrong is thistles and barbed wire rather than death by exposure. A mile of this is mental stimulation, 2 miles is tiresome, and 5 miles could put you on the bus back home.

This won't work very well in Wales, and it won't work at all in Scotland. England's mountains may be mostly rather little and titchy – but England's long paths and pink-line network, its field and forest, its moor and middle-sized hill, are altogether excellent for the improvised meander, the coast-to-coast stroll.

As your map eyes develop, you'll be able to pick out the path along the chalk escarpment or up inside the wooded ravine. A river's a guideline as well as pleasant company. Great is the satisfaction in tracking down a pretty bit of path from hints on the map: equally great the annoyance when you get it wrong and end up tangled in brambles on the banks of a footbridgeless ditch.

So walk two or three of the routes in this book – or even all eight of them. But then take compass and courage in hand, and venture into the unexplored interior of England.

right: Looking north-west from Sgurr nan Coireachan

Foot Notes

HOW TO USE THE DISTANCE CHARTS

One or two places listed are off-route (extra miles for the diversion in brackets). Unless otherwise indicated, centres listed have a food shop, and B&B or inn. (Listing 'YH' indicates Youth Hostel as well as other accommodation and shop – unless 'YH only'. However, 'Bothy' means bothy only.)

Village shops come and go – with more going than coming – and crucial ones should be confirmed with Tourist Information. Almost all main-road petrol stations now sell snack foods.

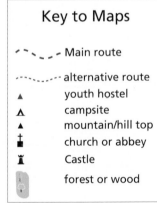

Key to Maps

- Main route
- alternative route
▲ youth hostel
Λ campsite
▲ mountain/hill top
♁ church or abbey
♔ Castle
forest or wood

FINDING FURTHER INFORMATION

The first source of information is the Tourist Information Centre. The large ones offer voicemail and brochures, but at the small local ones you'll find helpful people who know about buses, pubs and village shops.

Not every B&B is registered with the Tourist Board. Most libraries hold *Yellow Pages* for the whole country, and these can tell you about shops (grocers & convenience stores) and accommodation (hotels & inns; guest houses and B&Bs); and petrol stations (for those snack foods).

More and more useful information is now to be found on the internet. Websites like Wainwright's Coast-to-Coast (www.coast2coast.co.uk) and Offa's Dyke (www.offas-dyke.co.uk) may eventually replace paper information altogether. Updates and webchat on the routes of this book may be found on www.grey-stone.co.uk.

ACCOMMODATION

Youth hostels are marked on OS maps: they cost about £10 a night. Their phone numbers are in *Yellow Pages* (hostels); general information such as summer opening season from YHA,
8 St Stephen's Hill, St Albans, Herts AL1 2DY, tel: 01727 845 047 (www.yha-england-wales.org.uk). In Scotland, it's the SYHA, 7 Glebe Crescent, Stirling FK17 2JA; Central Reservations 08701 553255 or email reservations@ syha.org.uk.

Independent hostels are similar but less solemn, and allow alcohol. *Independent Hostel Guide UK and Ireland* about £4 from Backpackers' Press, 2 Rockview Cottages, Matlock, Bath DE4 3PG.

A free listing of *Independent Hostels Scotland* from Croft

Bunkhouse, 7 Portnalong, Isle of Skye IV47 8SL (www.hostel-scotland.co.uk) – they also publish a free public transport map of Scotland.

Bunkhouses may be simple sheds attached to hotels, or barns slightly adopted to accommodate humans (camping barns, at about £3); some are hostels under another name. Camping barns listing from YHA (see above).

WEATHER FORECASTS

0870 600 4242 for a roundup of Met Office premium rate telephone forecasts around the UK www.meto.govt.uk/home.html (Met Office homepage)
Scottish Winter weather: www.winterhighland.co.uk
Scottish Avalanche Information Service: 0800 0960 007

ACCESS

Access over upland and mountain areas is generally accepted, though not yet a legal right. Within England and Wales, access through lowland and farmland is on the rights of way marked on OS and Harveys maps. In Scotland and Ireland, lowland access is a matter of common sense, improvisation and politeness.

On heather moors, grouse shooting takes place from 12 August to 12 December. On most Scottish mountains, stag stalking is from mid-August to mid-October. Hill sheep are lambing from mid-April to the start of June, and this is also

nesting-time for moorland birds. Walkers at these times should be particularly considerate of the needs of other hill users, human or animal. Many Scottish estates have autumn phonelines where you can consult with the stalker.

Wild camping at high level, done inconspicuously and with consideration, is accepted in most of Scotland, upland Wales and the Lake District.

Heading for the Scottish Hills, from the Scottish Mountaineering Trust, is a handbook for stalking-season walkers. *Rights of Way: A Guide to the Law in Scotland* is published by the Scottish Rights of Way Society.

COAST-TO-COAST EVENTS

The Great Outdoor Challenge: coast-to-coast across Highland Scotland by whatever route you like in late May: the entry form is in the October issue of *TGO* magazine.

Highland Cross: Kintail to Beauly duathlon (half on bike) for teams of three.
HC Organisers, 19 Blackwell Road, Culloden IV2 7DZ

Across Ross Walk (64ml/100km Dingwall to Dornie):
Children 1st, 14 Kenneth St, Inverness IV3 5NR

Across Wales Walk (45ml/72km Anchor to Clarach Bay):
Stuart Lamb, 42 Hunt End Lane, Hunt End, Redditch B97 5UW

SKILLS & EQUIPMENT

Anyone undertaking one of these long routes should already be accustomed to single-day walks. Anyone undertaking one of the mountain routes should be accustomed to single-day mountain walks – in particular, should be able to navigate in foul weather and have some knowledge and experience of just how foul weather is likely to be. Most equipment and supplies can simply be carried over from normal daywalking.

Boots: should be comfortable, well worn in and not too heavy; 3-season leather boots are very suitable.

Socks are important. They should be expensive, new and gently hand-washed whenever you get the chance.

Rucksack: if you're backpacking you'll need a 65 to 75ltr sack. One of 45 to 55ltr will do if you're staying at B&Bs. A badly made or badly fitting sack adds 10lb (5kg) to the apparent load. Lowe Alpine and Berghaus are sound brands, but it's more important to get a sack that's right for your sex and back length. Many have adjustable backs: make the shop get this right for you before you buy. No rucksack is completely waterproof, so pack things in plastic bags inside.

Sleeping bag: 1-2 season rating is warm enough for late spring to early autumn, and will be nice and light. Expensive down ones have a superb warmth-to-weight ratio but must be kept dry.

Tent: If you intend to camp high in the mountains, make sure your tent is good enough. Older ridge tents need A-poles for stability in high winds. Dome tents with flexible poles are more stable than tunnel ones. Those by Terra Nova, Phoenix and North Face are among the best.

Even more weight can be saved by using a **bivvy bag**. In good weather this is nicer than a tent, and in bad weather it's a great deal nastier. It's worth wearing extra clothes in bed, and taking time to find a sheltered spot on insulating heather or old grasses.

For the impoverished walker, much better than a cheap tent is a basic bivvy at around £50 from Kathmandu Trekking – their bags are very nearly as effective as high-spec Goretex ones, at less than half the price.

Load, including two days' food, should not exceed 30lb (13kg). No little luxuries can justify the extra suffering as the load passes that point. Those in B&Bs should aim for a maximum of 20lb (9kg).

Food and drink: Food is heavy, so find out about all the shops along the way. 1kg (just over 2lb) will satisfy the need of a fit walker over a long day (4000 Cals). On the shorter and less fit first few days you could do with slightly less. If you look at 1kg and say 'I'll never eat all that', the answer is – try your best! Too little eating causes tiredness. Cold food carries the same energy as hot, and a cooker is a luxury. Not having the weight of the cooker on your back could be an even greater luxury.

Most walkers are happy to drink stream water above the 1000ft (300m) contour. Bacterial infection of hill streams isn't yet a serious problem in the UK. A litre bottle, empty most of the time, will tide you over dry patches. Water is more of a problem in farmland and countryside: 2lt a day may be too little in July heat. But you can always beg from householders.

SAFETY

Judgment and experience gained on shorter walks are your first safety precaution. Find out that your boots are too small, that your waterproofs aren't waterproof – get lost while learning to read maps – forget the blister plasters – all while still within four hours of your car.

Although the Highland and Grampian walk in particular is designed to be done without a tent, when something nasty happens a survival bag, bivvy bag or (for larger groups) a shared survival shelter does make the difference between life and death.

Even if you're in part of the hills where a mobile phone is effective, the accident that breaks your leg may well also break your phone. Leave with some sensible person a route-plan with scheduled phone-in points. If you don't know any sensible people, leave it with the police.

For Mountain Rescue call the Police on 999.

USEFUL BOOKS, WEBSITES AND ADDRESSES

Guidebooks for each of our eight walks are listed in the end-of-chapter Planning Panel

Long Distance Walkers' Handbook pb (A&C Black/LDWA) – all known long-distance trails, particularly in England; lists guidebooks for each route

OS Mapping Index (free) – marks all National Trails and many recreational paths

Channel to Channel by Ian &
Kay Sayer (p/b Kimberley Publishing)
Across Scotland on Foot by Ronald Turnbull (Grey Stone) – general coast-to-coast handbook with six routes

Scottish Hill Tracks (SRWS) – a guidebook to all the long-distance rights-of-way of Scotland

Various Glens of Scotland books by Peter D. Koch-Osborne (all p/b Cicerone) – low-level through routes

West Highland Walks 1 – 3 and *Highland Walks: Deeside* by Hamish MacInnes (p/b Hodder) – more low-level through routes, and shorter walks

Exploring Scottish Hill Tracks by Ralph Storer (p/b Little Brown)

100 Best Routes on Scottish Mountains by Ralph Storer (p/b Little Brown) – a roundup of hills worth diverting your route over

High Mountains of Britain & Ireland by Irvine Butterfield (p/b Bâton Wicks) – standard routes up all 3000-footers

OS Maps: www.ordsvy.gov.uk

Harveys Maps: www.harveymaps.co.uk

Long Distance Walkers' Association: J Chapman, 63 Yockley Close, The Maultway, Camberley GU15 1QQ

Ramblers' Association: www.ramblers.org.uk

Mountain Bothies Association: David Askew, Johnson Farm House, Johnby, Penrith CA11 0VV

ACKNOWLEDGEMENTS

John thanks those who have been good company on the hills: his wife Nicola on Lakeland to Lindisfarne and Offa's Dyke, Roy Clayton on Snowdonia to Gower. The two authors thank each other for comradeship on Beauly to Applecross. Thanks to the folk of the Offa's Dyke Association and the various bodies who maintain Wainwright's walk: their hard work ensures two fine paths with no obstructions.

We dedicate the book to the overnight stopping-points: the wardens of the YHA and SYHA, and of the independent hostels; the labourers of the Mountain Bothies Association; the innkeepers, the ladies (and occasional gentlemen) of the B&Bs; and various of our friends and family. How would we walk without them? It is dedicated too in memory of Genny Turnbull, who provided shelter on Uphill to Old Harry.

Index